English Country Furniture

THE VERNACULAR TRADITION

DAVID KNELL

SHIRE PUBLICATIONS LTD

COVER: Ash and elm comb-back Windsor chair from the Thames Valley, mid eighteenth century.

ACKNOWLEDGEMENTS

I am deeply indebted to all those whose research has contributed to the present state of knowledge; some of the published material is listed in the bibliography.

I am particularly grateful to Sotheby's for so generously providing a large proportion of the photographs, including the cover picture. The kind help of Samantha Georgeson and Kirsty Knight is warmly appreciated. In addition, my thanks are due to Andrew Mardell, who took many of the other photographs.

Further acknowledgements for illustrations are as follows: City of Birmingham Public Libraries, page 18; Bonham's, pages 80, 89; Brasenose College, Oxford, page 12; Mrs W. Carmichael, pages 50, 58; Christie's, page 87; Dr B.D. Cotton, page 80; Vicki Emery, pages 20, 94; Derek Green, page 69; Mrs E. Hand, page 17; Paul Hopwell Antiques, page 46; John Humphry, page 14; Institute of Agricultural History and Museum of English Rural Life, University of Reading, pages 11, 94; H.W. Keil Ltd, pages 38, 42, 79; Leeds City Art Galleries, page 27; Brian Loomes, pages 84, 86; Phillips, page 4; Miss S. Ryder, pages 11, 29, 35; Oswald Simpson, page 81; Spencer's, Retford, page 37; Tennant's, North Yorkshire, pages 3, 95; Up Country, Tunbridge Wells, pages 37, 40, 91; Michael Wakelin and Helen Linfield, pages 41, 44, 52, 74, 78, 82; Mrs E. Williams, page 96; Clare Wilson, pages 16, 57; Robert Young Antiques, pages 66, 74, 79.

Printed in Great Britain by CIT Printing Services, Press Buildings, Merlins Bridge, Haverfordwest, Dyfed SA61 1XF.

CONTENTS

An oak high dresser, 1770-1800. This dresser came from Field House, near Sowerby Bridge, West Yorkshire, and the arrangement of a pair of cupboard doors surrounded by drawers is typical of many examples from this region. It is a formal type of dresser and stood in a grand upstairs hallway, where it was used to display fine china and store bed linen, rather than performing a more utilitarian function in the kitchen.

An early eighteenth-century oak bureau bearing the label of John Gatehouse, a London cabinet-maker. Evidence such as this bureau refutes the belief that ordinary oak furniture was invariably provincial and highlights the inaccuracy of 'country' as an overall generic term.

INTRODUCTION

Conventional histories of English furniture have been largely based on pieces which furnished the manors and mansions of the richer classes and thus tend towards a qualitative rather than a truly representative analysis. The vast bulk of old English furniture, that of ordinary people, has, with the exception of examples antedating 1700, been virtually ignored by serious historians until quite recently. A wider consideration of furniture as part of social history rather than merely as supreme examples of cabinet-making skill or as art objects has led to a reappraisal of the merits of humbler pieces and these are now increasingly seen as vital to a properly balanced view of *epiplatology* (the study of furniture and interior decor through the ages).

Certain types of furniture — settles, dressers, rush-seated chairs, cricket tables and so on — were specifically suited to the modest homes of working people and evolved more or less independently of the formal furnishings of richer houses. Even those inferior grades of furniture whose form and basic style are clearly derivative often tend to evince a decidedly 'provincial' character in terms of material, finish and constructional and decorative details and they frequently include idiosyncratic regional traits which are not related to the mainstream patterns. Nevertheless, there can be no *precise* parameters defining what is loosely termed vernacular or popular furniture as a distinct class. While the opposite extremes of superior and inferior furniture are manifestly different, a considerable overlap exists in the middle ground. 'Vernacular' implies a native, normally unsophisticated, product of ordinary people but its application is open to wide interpretation and, in the case of furniture at least, the term cannot be restricted only to its narrower sense of describing articles made exclusively from indigenous material. Imported timbers such as continental oak, pine and even mahogany were commonly used for humbler pieces conforming to local and traditional idioms. The period over which vernacular furniture was made is similarly free of clear definition; more modest forms of furniture were made for the medieval peasant as they were for the Victorian factory worker. The greater concentration on later pieces is guided by purely practical reasons; very little furniture of the lower classes survives from before the eighteenth century. (Most of the extant carved oak furniture of the sixteenth and seventeenth centuries belonged originally to the more affluent members of society.)

The common umbrella term 'country furniture' is patently inaccurate.

'Card Castles' by the Cheshire artist W. H. Midwood, dated 1871. Furniture of different periods and varying quality is mixed in this cottage interior. Tea is being served on a joined gateleg table of the early eighteenth century by a woman seated on a Liverpool turned chair of the early nineteenth century. The carved crest of a seventeenth-century joined armchair has been recycled to adorn the foot of the relatively crude boarded cradle on the right. A brass-dial longcase clock stands against the back wall. Note the use of a makeshift bed (left) in this primary downstairs room.

Although before the nineteenth century over three-quarters of the English population lived in the countryside, much of their furniture was indistinguishable from that belonging to people of the same class living in large towns and cities. Indeed, recent research has confirmed that for sound commercial reasons the manufacture of many well-known types of so-called 'country' furniture was frequently based in towns and in larger trading conurbations, which served not only the local area but sometimes other distant parts of the region.

Nor are descriptions such as 'cottage', 'farmhouse' or 'provincial' any more satisfactory as overall terms for everyday furniture. The first two are too restrictive and the last is misleading: it is clear that, despite the powers of trade guilds and companies, a great deal of humble furniture was made by workshops situated either very near or within London. It is also evident that many of even the finest London cabinet-makers made furniture in different grades of quality according to what customers could afford — expensive pieces in fine imported timbers and veneers for their richer patrons, and an 'economy' range of lesser pieces in a basically similar style but made in plain oak for their less affluent clients.

Perhaps the only major characteristic that unifies the furniture dealt with in this book is its relatively low cost at the time of manufacture. Its simple materials and comparative lack of sophistication are merely inconstant reflections of this. Nevertheless, such enforced frugality often had a happy result. The overriding constraints of economic manufacture and utilitarian use imposed a design discipline which eschewed excessive ornamentation and concentrated more on basic form and line. The undeniable aesthetic appeal of so much vernacular furniture was because of, rather than despite, its very limitations.

An oak corner cupboard of c.1800, probably from the Lancashire/Cheshire region. Note the pronounced medullary rays on the doors. The carcase members framing the doors have been veneered in mahogany — a particularly common practice in the north of England. The shell inlays on the door panels and the parquetry banding on the frieze would not have been made by the joiner himself but bought from a wholesale supplier and applied.

Timber and Construction

The use of imported hardwoods, such as mahogany, became increasingly widespread in the production of fine furniture during the eighteenth century but, since such timber tended to be expensive, furniture intended for popular use was largely made from native hardwoods and imported softwoods. Hardwoods (angiosperms and normally deciduous in temperate climates) in common use included alder, ash, beech, chestnut, elm, maple, oak and the fruitwoods (apple, cherry, pear and plum). Softwoods (conifers and usually evergreen) included not only the varieties of true pine but also fir, larch, spruce and indigenous yew.

Oak has been particularly revered ever since the middle ages and William Harrison, the Elizabethan topographer, asserted that in house-building 'nothing but oke [was] any whit regarded'. From the middle ages onwards, native timber was supplemented by supplies from abroad, oak from continental Europe (or *wainscot*) being widely favoured for its comparatively straight growth and a marked tendency to display an attractive range of medullary ray patterns. Prominent medullary rays, that is, radial markings caused by groups of storage cells in the tree, are particularly characteristic of oak and, depending on treatment, are normally either darker or paler than the surrounding wood. Oak was undoubtedly the preferred timber of the middle classes before the eighteenth century and since oak is exceptionally durable, hardening with age and resistant to both rot and woodworm, a large proportion of early furniture made from it has survived.

Ash and *elm* were also in wide use from medieval times. Both have grain markings superficially similar to those of oak, though without medullary rays, and both were valued for their toughness. Ash was widely used for turned and Windsor chairs. Since it can be steam-bent, it was particularly suitable for bowed members such as arms and backs. Elm was valued for its resistance to damp and was typically used for the seats of Windsor chairs because its cross-grained growth prevents it from splitting when bored. Its worst characteristic is an unfortunate tendency to warp.

Pine has become a fairly loose term which can refer to several other members of the Pinaceae family in addition to the true pines of the *Pinus* genus. *Deal* is largely synonymous and is derived from an old German term meaning a portion, an allusion to the sawn planks imported in large quantities from northern Europe during the middle ages. Pine was highly regarded at that time — it was ordered by Henry III for panelling at Winchester Castle and by Henry VIII for Nonsuch Palace — but evidence suggests that it was also used in much humbler contexts at least as early as the sixteenth century. With the British colonisation of North America during the seventeenth and eighteenth centuries, European pine was supplemented by enormous supplies from this newer source. The increasing availability of pine and the increasing price of hardwood after the French wars of 1793-1815 combined to establish deal as the universal choice for the cheap mass-produced furniture of the nineteenth century.

Methods of furniture construction not only varied according to the type of furniture being produced — the skills required to make a turned chair are entirely different to those for a chest of drawers — but also were influenced by interrelated factors such as the market, the materials available locally, regional traditions and the location and scale of the workshop. At one extreme, one man (a Windsor chairmaker, for instance) might be responsible for making a piece from start to finish, from cutting the trees to applying the final paint or stain. At the other extreme, he might be only a link in a long chain, assembling parts supplied by other workers and then handing them on to be finished by someone else. Such specialisation in one stage of the work was typical of many firms making Windsor chairs in the High Wycombe area.

The creation of even a fairly simple piece of storage furniture normally called for contributions from several specialists. The timber was initially cut by the sawyer; members such as legs or stretchers were possibly ornamented by the turner; the piece was assembled by the carpenter or joiner; and final decoration was perhaps executed by a separate carver or painter. The different items of metal hardware, although perhaps supplied by a single ironmonger, might well have originated in the workshops of various makers: the nailsmith, blacksmith, locksmith, brassfounder and so on.

A rural craftsman might have to master several trades in order to eke out a living. Adam Smith, the economist, noted in 1776 that 'A country carpenter ... is not only a carpenter, but a joiner, a cabinet-maker, and even a carver in wood, as well as a wheel-wright, a plough-wright, a cart and waggon maker'. Indeed, the latter trades might well be far more important in an agricultural community and the making of furniture merely an occasional sideline of his business. In larger towns, however, the different trades were likely to be clearly defined and it was sometimes

The cheaper grades of Victorian storage furniture were typically of pine and painted to resemble a superior timber. This pine chest of drawers of the second half of the nineteenth century was found in south-eastern England and bears a simulated curly maple finish. White ceramic knobs were popular from 1850 onwards.

Left: An elm dug-out chair from Shropshire, probably late eighteenth to early nineteenth century. A naturally hollow tree trunk has been roughly shaped and a seat and armrests have been added.
Right: A nineteenth-century sycamore stool of wedged construction. The legs are merely chamfered rather than turned on a lathe.

Above: A turned chair shown in an English woodcut of 1563. It is without arms and is evidently of the four-post (rather than triangular) type. The seat may have been made of leather, wood or rushes.

Left: A turned ash armchair made in the Lancashire/Cheshire region, probably in the first half of the nineteenth century. The seat is woven from rushes.

illegal for a craftsman to put his hand to a craft other than his own. Some urban firms were very large indeed — George Seddon, a London cabinet-maker, is recorded as employing over four hundred workers in 1786 — and each craftsman normally specialised in only one aspect of manufacture.

One of the most elementary ways of fashioning timber to create a simple receptacle, requiring neither carpentry nor joinery skills, is the *dug-out* method, whereby the central portion of a log is laboriously hollowed out, leaving the outer surfaces as base and sides and the severed top as a lid. Several ancient examples of this form have survived as chests in churches, although a few are somewhat later than they may at first appear and the technique seems to have persisted possibly into the seventeenth century. Some extant chairs were also created by using hollow logs and seating of this kind was still being made in the early nineteenth century.

Another basic construction method was that used in *wedged* (or *primitive*) furniture, familiar from the illustrations in medieval manuscripts and in the traditional workaday stools and benches of more recent times. Essentially, the method is based on a central slab (a seat or table top) into which whittled stake-like members are wedged to create legs and uprights. The member is deeply notched at one end, the notched end is rammed through the appropriate hole in the slab and a wooden wedge hammered into the notch to hold the member firmly in place. The protruding wedged end of the member is then cut off flush with the slab surface. Such furniture presented itself as the obvious choice of the poorer classes; the necessary timber was readily available at no cost, the requisite tools (axe, adze, knife and auger) were to be found in nearly every rural home and the skills needed were minimal.

The turner's lathe, like the potter's wheel, is one of the oldest forms of machinery and the products of both are described as 'thrown', an Old English term for 'turned'. In addition to providing a more sophisticated means of producing members for wedged and joined furniture, turnery was widely used for complete items, although the range was necessarily constrained by the limitations of the technique. The commonest examples of furniture made entirely by a turner are chairs and stools.

The practice of making furniture by simply fixing planks of wood together by means of nails or wooden pegs is associated with the trade of carpentry and is known as *boarded* or *plank* construction. The method is undoubtedly easy and cheap but its products are restricted to fairly

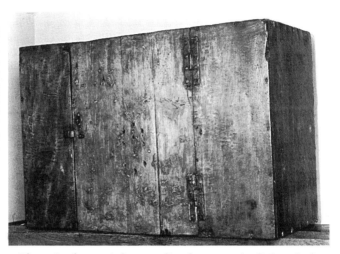

A boarded elm food cupboard of the eighteenth century in which the planks are merely nailed together. The pine door is pierced in a simple pattern for ventilation.

box-like forms. There is also an inherent disadvantage in fixing timber rigidly across its grain; as the wood shrinks or warps with age, the inhibiting nails or pegs cause it to split.

A more advanced method of furniture construction is that of joinery, in which, instead of nails, interlocking portions are cut on the wood itself. The chief joint is the mortise-and-tenon, made by inserting a tongue, or *tenon* (usually rectangular), made on the end of one member into a corresponding cavity, or *mortise*, excavated in the side of the other. Invariably on all furniture made before 1700 and frequently on furniture made until about 1850, the joint was strengthened by one or two pegs inserted into holes drilled right through both mortise and tenon. The hole in the tenon was drilled slightly closer to the shoulder than the corresponding hole in the mortise so that when the peg was driven home the two pieces of wood were drawn tightly together.

Although much used in medieval house-building, the mortise-and-tenon joint does not appear to have been widely applied to English furniture until the fifteenth century, when it was commonly used in the

A tenon. The hole for the peg can be clearly seen.

A joined oak chest, probably West Country 1630-80. All members are held by mortise-and-tenon joints, including the panelled lid and ends.

This seventeenth-century oak chest combines a superior joined and panelled front with a plank lid and boarded ends. It should not be regarded as a transitional form but merely as an economic alternative to chests which were wholly joined.

framework of panelling. Joined furniture is not only stronger than that which is boarded but also proportionally lighter in weight and, since panels are simply held in place by grooves in the frame rather than being fixed by nails or glue, far less likely to split. The main vertical members of a piece of panelled furniture (the four corner posts of a chest, for instance) are generally known as *stiles*, into which the horizontal *rails* are tenoned. Shorter vertical members which tenon into rails at top and bottom are termed *muntins*.

Another joint used in medieval house-building was the *single dovetail*, basically a wedge-shaped tenon which fits into a mortise of corresponding shape. *Multiple dovetailing* consists of a series of dovetails and intermediate *pins* (see illustration) cut on the ends of wide boards so that the boards interlock when joined at right angles. Although occasionally found on much earlier pieces (a dovetailed chest of the late fourteenth

Left: A dovetailed elm chest of the early nineteenth century.
Right: Detail of the elm chest. The dovetails are formed from the left-hand board (the chest end). The wedge-shaped projections of the right-hand board (the chest front) that fit in the spaces, or eyes, between the dovetails are known as 'pins'.

century survives at Haddon Hall in Derbyshire), multiple dovetailing does not appear to have become widespread in the making of English furniture until the second half of the seventeenth century. In *open* or *through dovetailing* the ends of the joining members show on both sides of the angle. In *concealed* or *lapped dovetailing* the cavities that receive the wedges are not cut right through, thus preserving one unmarked surface. Lapped dovetailing was ideal for the fronts of drawers, where it was desirable to conceal the construction.

Once a piece of furniture had been made, the bare wood was normally treated in some way for both practical and aesthetic reasons. Transparent finishes such as oil and beeswax afforded some protection from decay while enhancing the natural beauty of the timber. Varnish (basically a suspension of gum or resin in a solvent) was used from at least the seventeenth century and imparted a hard-wearing surface. Cheaper timbers, especially pine, were often stained to resemble a more expensive wood. Paint was also frequently used for this purpose; a surprisingly realistic woodgrain effect could be achieved by *scumbling*, the partial removal of a dark 'scum' or glaze by means of a comb, brush or feather before it had dried, thus revealing streaks of the paler base paint. Other materials could be simulated in the same way; a marble effect was considered appropriate for fire surrounds and the top surfaces of wash-stands. Fantastic finishes, not based on any real material, could be invented and used purely for decorative effect. It is a great pity that so much of this work has been destroyed forever by the recent fad for stripping pine furniture.

Apart from these simulation finishes, the typical paint finish was plain monochrome — red, brown and green or blue-green appear to have been the commonest — and, while striping and simple abstract patterns are frequently found on nineteenth-century pieces, more dramatic polychrome themes are rare on English vernacular furniture.

Since timber predominates, the seemingly minor contributions to a piece of furniture provided by metalworkers in the form of nails, screws, hinges, locks, catches and so on are sometimes overlooked. But, if demonstrably original, such items are highly significant and, when properly considered with other factors, may well supply some important clues to dating. Early nails were forged by hand and were normally square or rectangular in section, tapering on all sides to a sharp point. Machine-cut nails, which generally taper on only two sides and are blunt, were not introduced in England until 1790 and the modern wire nail, with a cylindrical shank and a flat head, not until about 1890. Screws were quite widely used by 1720 and were being made by machine towards the end of the eighteenth century. Early machine-made screws superficially resemble those made entirely by hand since they were often

Left: A nineteenth-century boxed set of steel combs for use in scumbling.

Right: This winged settle (English or Welsh, late eighteenth or early nineteenth century) exhibits a striking use of paint. While the framing members bear a conventional grained scumble, the panels and end boards are decorated with a more dramatic cable pattern.

manually filed to finish them and they have the same style of flat head with a V-section slot. Nevertheless, screws made by machine before about 1850 tend to have less taper than their hand-made counterparts and are less likely to be pointed.

Early furniture fittings were mainly wooden or iron. Brass was very seldom used for handles or keyhole escutcheons before 1660 but, inspired by the fittings on the oriental cabinets which became increasingly popular at that time, brass hardware became fashionable during the late seventeenth century and the patterns were based directly on Chinese prototypes. Although cheap iron fittings were often substituted on unimportant furniture, brass hardware remained as the preferred choice until a vogue for wooden knobs dominated in the nineteenth century. During the Victorian period wooden knobs were supplemented by glass and ceramic varieties.

Contrary to a common belief, wrought-iron fittings were not always bought from a local blacksmith. Large wholesalers could supply an enormous assortment of hardware, such as the hinges advertised by this Birmingham firm in 1835. Note the persistence of butterfly, H and HL hinges into the nineteenth century.

IDENTIFICATION: REGION AND DATE

The cultural differences between one part of England and another derive from ethnic, geographic and economic variations and are clearly manifested in the traditional customs, crafts and products of more or less distinct regions. Before the enormous improvements in communications, transport and the national distribution of mass-produced goods in the late nineteenth century, those differences were far more marked than they are today. The effects of those differences on local vernacular architecture have long been noted but the extent to which those same idiosyncrasies were also reflected in the design, material, construction and decorative details of the furniture within those buildings has been recognised only relatively recently. Indeed, a systematic analysis and collation of those variations is even more recent and research is as yet still very much in its infancy.

Unlike buildings, which normally remain in the place where they were made, most furniture is by its nature movable; consequently, discovering where a piece was made can be complex and problematic. There is sometimes direct evidence. Occasionally a piece still bears the trade label or stamp of its maker or is inscribed under a drawer or in some other inconspicuous place. Sometimes a chest or a drawer is lined with old newspaper, which may provide some clues to region and date. In many cases a piece of furniture has a long association with a particular family or locality. However, all these sources of information must be treated with great caution; labels and inscriptions may be misleading and have nothing to do with the maker; newspaper linings may have been added later, far from where the piece was made; and even a centuries-old association with a certain place is not always indisputable proof of origin.

Moreover, most extant furniture has neither a maker's mark nor the benefit of a secure provenance. Generally, therefore, identification must rely on less direct methods. The conventional method, which can sometimes determine both region and date, is based on a close comparison of the example in question with similar yet firmly identified pieces of furniture and with the constructional or decorative details of fixed architectural woodwork. In addition, the sheer frequency with which a certain type or feature may occur in one region may provide some grounds for tentative attribution, particularly when characteristics appear to be peculiar to that district and when comparative analysis reveals shared trends. Examples can thus occasionally be identified with some confidence even when entirely remote from their original context.

A joined oak chest found in West Yorkshire. Mitred mouldings are applied to the panels and to the pair of drawers. The top rail bears the punched inscription: + SOLOMON + HVTSON + MADE + ME + 1673 + SH +.

Since applying scientific techniques is normally impractical, expensive or inapplicable, the dating of most pieces of anonymous furniture must, for the time being at least, remain largely empirical. Date attribution must be based on a collective consideration of four main factors: the latest constructional or decorative feature; the likely regional source; the degree of originality; and the indications of authenticity. The identification of the very latest (and demonstrably original) constructional or decorative feature will provide the very earliest date that a piece could have been made.

An oak settle similar to that shown on page 83, having fielded panels to the back and cabriole legs on the front, but with a triple-reeded

A clue to both the regional origin and the approximate date of this anonymous boarded box (with original red paint) is provided by the internal lining — an Oxford newspaper dated 1810.

moulding (a band of parallel convex ridges) along the top, can be offered as an example: plain fielded panels suggest a date after 1660; cabriole legs developed into a mature form around 1710 and were highly fashionable during the middle of the eighteenth century; but the triple-reeded moulding, the latest feature, would indicate that the settle is unlikely to have been made before about 1800. All parts of the settle, including the moulding, are carefully examined to confirm that they are original components rather than later additions. The style of the settle suggests that its regional source was the Cheshire and south Lancashire area and, since settles with archaic features such as fielded panels and cabriole legs were still being produced in this region in the early nineteenth century, the date indicated by the moulding is perfectly consistent with manufacture after 1800.

Left: Despite a lack of provenance, this turned chair of the second half of the nineteenth century can safely be attributed a Lancashire origin since it is of a distinctive type which constantly recurs in that region (occasionally bearing an identifiable maker's stamp) and appears to be peculiar to it. Note the late retention of a Sheraton back form and the archaic pad feet to the front legs.

Right: Archaic features, such as the base form of this oak chair, can be misleading and commonly lead to erroneously early date attributions. However, bases of this kind were still being produced in some regions during the second half of the eighteenth century. A close analysis of all features and a careful comparison with other datable chairs of its class suggest that this example was made between 1720 and 1770.

Many of the features seen in this oak low dresser from north-western England were introduced during the eighteenth century, but the reeded moulding (in this case quadruple) around the top suggests that it was probably made after 1800.

Modern research and common sense have tended to challenge many of the date attributions that were widely accepted in the past. Until the 1990s, for instance, it was popularly believed that American furniture styles of the eighteenth century lagged far behind British fashion. Such a notion is soon seen as highly implausible, however, when it is considered that even the slowest transatlantic voyage in the eighteenth century took only a number of weeks, not decades. While their interest in the most avant-garde pieces for British aristocrats was naturally limited, American makers did pride themselves in keeping abreast of the newest trends in more ordinary furniture. The truth is not that the dates given for American vernacular furniture are particularly late, but rather that those commonly assigned to similar English pieces are often too early. It is evident that American and English pieces of the same type, style and class are likely to be roughly contemporary and that humbler examples of both are normally more traditional and conservative than superficially comparable furniture made for the very rich.

It is clear too that, far from consistently conforming to the chronological sequence of ordered evolution suggested by many earlier furniture historians, vernacular and, occasionally, even fine furniture was heavily influenced not only by the idiosyncrasies of regional pressures but sometimes also by those of individual workshop and personal preferences. Any universal set of rules by which furniture can ostensibly be dated from an examination of stylistic, decorative or constructional features must, therefore, be at best enormously generalised and simplistic; each piece is best considered as closely as possible within its own context. In the absence of a secure chronological reference (documentary evidence, for example) date attributions must stay broad and tentative.

The detection of major alterations and faking in antique furniture has become a specialised field but a few of the more salient points should be mentioned here. Complete fakes of later vernacular furniture are rare. Nevertheless, the utilitarian nature of such furniture ensured rough use and it is inevitable that much of it, even if genuinely old, will have been heavily repaired to prolong its useful life. In addition, pieces were sometimes altered in times gone by in order to bring them up to date (for instance, the replacement of brass handles by wooden knobs or bracket feet by turned feet in Victorian times) or, in more recent days, in order to enhance their value to collectors.

Perhaps the most significant clue to the true age of an apparently old piece of furniture lies in the condition of the timber. An absence of wear in those places where it should naturally have occurred will obviously arouse suspicion that the piece is not as old as it appears. Conversely, wear where it would not be expected might well indicate deliberate faking.

On the more visible exterior surfaces the timber will have normally acquired a patina made up of old varnish, wax, dirt and polish. The effect can be simulated superficially but a genuine patina created gradually over one or more centuries is highly distinctive. Under close examina-

Left: The irregular marks of a hand saw or pit saw can be clearly seen underneath this early nineteenth-century oak drop-leaf table.

Right: The underside of a nineteenth-century pine drawer, showing the regular curved marks left by a mechanical circular saw.

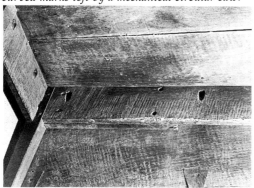

A boarded elm chest from the West Country, dated 1692. The series of notches on the ends of the front board is a common form of decoration on furniture of this type and helps to protect the vulnerable end grain.

tion, the scratch marks and grain will often be seen to stand slightly proud of the surface where wax and dirt have become caught and hardened into tiny ridges. The unpolished timber of rear and interior surfaces can be equally revealing. Bare and untreated wood darkens with time, usually to a distinctive shade of dirty greyish brown. Since the colour and condition of adjacent timber members can be expected to be reasonably uniform on an original piece of old furniture, later repairs or alterations made from newer wood should be readily exposed.

The saw marks visible on unplaned interior surfaces can be a guide to the probable date of manufacture. The timber used in early furniture was normally sawn manually over a pit and the saw marks are fairly rough and irregular. Since sawmills did not become well established in England until the late eighteenth century, the regular parallel marks of a mechanical frame saw generally indicate a date after that time. Similarly, the mechanical circular saw, although patented as early as 1777, did not come into widespread use until the first half of the nineteenth century and the curved marks left by it suggest a comparatively late date of manufacture.

CHESTS, BOXES AND DESKS

A large proportion of the chests surviving from medieval times are of a distinctive form of simple joined construction, known as *clamped front*, in which continuous tenons on the ends of the large horizontal front and back boards slot into grooves on the edges of the four wide corner stiles. The end boards, normally inset and canted, are held in a similar manner. The use of the clamped-front method persisted into the seventeenth century in the construction of robust grain or dough bins, generally termed *arks* in the north of England and *hutches* in the south.

The simplest chests were of boarded construction and this type must have been by far the most common in ordinary homes during the middle ages and, in one form or another, at least up to the nineteenth century. The boarded chest is essentially made from six boards, five of them being nailed or pegged together to create a box and the sixth one hinged on top to form the lid. In order to preserve the chest and its contents from damp and vermin, the end boards were often fixed with their grain vertical and carried down below the main body of the chest to keep it raised off the floor. Shaped wooden brackets, or *spandrels*, were sometimes added to the front for decorative effect. Feet could be formed by simply shaping the bases of the end boards. Carved decoration, if any, followed prevailing trends. Carving of a medieval character, sometimes in imitation of Gothic tracery, gradually gave way during the sixteenth century to a fashionable tendency to incorporate one or two of the classical motifs popularised during the Renaissance: fluting, lunettes and the guilloche were perennial favourites. By the second quarter of the eighteenth century plainness had become the general rule and carving was limited mainly to inscriptions or the occasional flourish.

There is some evidence to suggest that boarded chests were often specifically referred to as *coffers* in the past to distinguish them from those chests which were of joined construction. A stricter interpretation of the word 'coffer', however, asserts that it should properly be restricted to describe only those receptacles having domed lids, usually the product of a 'coffermaker' and covered in studded leather or cloth.

Superior chests of joined and panelled construction became increasingly common after the fifteenth century but owing to their comparatively high cost they were for some time limited mainly to the homes of the middle classes and above. Occasionally, however, the decorative schemes of panelled chests are imitated on cheaper boarded types in

A boarded pine chest with a single drawer mounted in the base, typical of many found in southeastern England. There are traces of the original red paint finish and the date '1766' is delineated in iron studs on the front board.

order to convey the same effect. Domestic chests made by either method were used primarily for storing clothing, bedding and linen and are frequently mentioned in early inventories as standing in such appropriate places as an upstairs landing or at the foot of a bed. Many of the boarded and most of the joined chests have a lidded compartment, or *till*, mounted internally at one end, in which valuables or other smaller items could be kept.

The most inconvenient aspect of chest storage, that of having to disturb the entire contents in order to reach an item kept at the bottom, was overcome by providing one or more unlidded boxes, or *drawers*, which could be withdrawn from the front. Chests which are fitted with only one or two drawers in the base but which are otherwise conventional were made from the sixteenth century up to the nineteenth and this type, the so-called *mule chest*, has become popularly associated with the keeping of a bride's dowry, although there is no reason to suppose that this kind of chest fulfilled such a function any more than those which had no drawers. The *chest of drawers* proper (that is, a chest completely composed of drawers which are not enclosed by doors and without a lidded compartment on top) had appeared by the middle of the seventeenth century. Since access to a chest of drawers did not depend upon a hinged lid, there was no reason to limit its height and from about 1680 they were frequently placed on separate stands, lending them a more imposing appearance. In the early eighteenth century the *chest on chest*, essentially

Left: A chest of drawers (oak, elm and fruitwood) from Carrow Abbey, Norwich, 1740-90. The arrangement of two shallow drawers flanked by two deep drawers in the upper part is an East Anglian feature. All the main drawers have a projecting lip moulding. The press mounted on top provided a convenient means of storing linen while keeping it neatly pressed at the same time.

Right: An oak chest on stand, 1740-90. The drawers have a cock bead round their edges and are crossbanded in yew. A northern origin is suggested by the boldness and complexity of the cornice and medial mouldings. The 'broken' pediment, if original, is an unusual feature on English examples.

one chest of drawers mounted on top of another, gained favour. It was a development which offered the attractive advantage of greatly increasing storage capacity without taking up any further floor space. Nevertheless, both the expense of such furniture and the height of ceilings restricted the use of tall chests in smaller houses and even normal chests of drawers were sometimes constructed so that they could divide into two sections to enable them to be taken up or down winding staircases.

More or less subtle differences in the construction and decorative treatment of drawers and of the carcase members framing them can offer some indication of date. Until about 1730 drawers are often suspended by means of strips of wood nailed inside the carcase which fit horizontal channels cut on the drawer sides. The alternative method, that of allowing the drawer to slide on its base (or applied runners on more sophisticated work), was in use earlier and regained favour during the late seventeenth century, eventually becoming the standard arrangement up to the present day. Stuart drawers tend to have their fronts ornamented with mouldings applied in geometric patterns, a fashion which continued up to about 1730 or even later in some areas. By the late seventeenth century, however, oriental styles were exerting a strong influence on European furniture design and it was becoming increasingly fashionable to make drawers resemble their Far Eastern counterparts. The use of concealed dovetailing allowed the drawer fronts to be left plain, and half-round or double half-round mouldings were often applied to the framing members in imitation of the convex-fronted drawer divisions inside oriental cabinets.

During the early eighteenth century two new styles emerged. The first, which appeared around 1710, was an *ovolo lip moulding*, either flush or projecting around the perimeter of each drawer front and hiding the gap between drawer and carcase, the carcase itself being left flat-faced. The second style, introduced by 1725, was a *cock bead*, an edging strip applied round the drawer front which stood slightly proud of the surface but which, unlike the projecting variety of lip moulding, did not overlap the carcase. Towards the end of the eighteenth century both methods were occasionally dispensed with altogether and both the drawer front and the carcase were simply left flush. It is this plain and somewhat severe style which is most commonly encountered on the mass-produced pine chests of drawers of the nineteenth century. Chest feet also conformed roughly to an overlapping chronological sequence. The bracket foot, a protruding right-angled foot inspired by oriental types, became almost universal after 1700. The French rococo foot, flush with the carcase, sometimes splayed and linked by shaped aprons, was fashionable during the neo-classical period in the late eighteenth and early nineteenth centuries and a turned foot, based on classical design, was widely favoured from the early nineteenth century onwards.

Oak storage furniture of the eighteenth and early nineteenth centuries frequently has flush areas, such as drawer fronts, panels and doors, bordered by *crossbanding*, a narrow inlay of veneer (normally a fine

A pine chest of drawers found in Sussex; second half of the nineteenth century. This example retains its original paint finish, a dark over pale brown scumble which is intended to represent mahogany.

This pine chest (second half of the nineteenth century) is typical of those used by seamen to store their belongings on board ship. It became a tradition for the owner to paint a nautical scene on the underside of the lid. Since it was more vulnerable to wear and damage, the exterior of the chest was normally left plain; this example bears a conventional scumble finish.

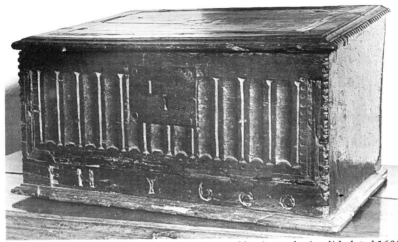

A portable oak desk of boarded construction and having a sloping lid, dated 1600. The fluting carved on the front surface was one of the classical motifs that became very popular from the sixteenth century onwards.

timber such as mahogany) set with its grain at right angles to the edge. In some (mainly northern) regions the crossbanding is sometimes inset about 1-3 cm from the edge.

Seventeenth- and eighteenth-century flat-lidded boxes with carved decoration have survived in large numbers and, despite the popular use of a Victorian term, *Bible box*, to describe them, they were undoubtedly used for the storage of many other smaller items: clothing accessories, sewing equipment, documents, writing materials and so on. Indeed, it is likely that very few of these boxes were specifically made to hold only a Bible. Most are of boarded construction, though joined examples are occasionally found and dovetailing became common for the plain boxes of the eighteenth and nineteenth centuries.

A large proportion of the plain pine chests and boxes of the nineteenth century, often fitted with a carrying handle at each end and obviously suited to travelling, would have been intended as *lodging boxes*. The box and its contents would have constituted the only possessions carried by adolescents when leaving home to go into farmwork, domestic service or apprenticeships. As such, they may well have provided the only storage, seat and table in sparsely furnished staff accommodation. Names and dates are occasionally found inscribed on them and those chests belonging to seamen sometimes include scenes, appropriately nautical, painted on the undersides of their lids.

Since domestic lidded desks are in essence merely a specialised extension of the box principle, they may be considered in the same chapter. It
is a reflection of the growth of literacy during the late sixteenth and
seventeenth centuries that even relatively modest homes would occasionally be furnished with a box having a sloping lid — a simple desk.
Being portable, such desks were either placed on the nearest convenient
table or rested on the user's lap. They were often provided with internal
shelves and drawers and, if raised slightly, the sloping lid, apart from
being at a convenient angle for reading or writing, allowed access to the
interior without disturbing everything on it. Towards the end of the
seventeenth century the practice of mounting the desk on a purpose-built
stand became common. Better examples of the type had the lid, or *fall*,
hinged at the base instead of at the top and supported by a pair of
extractable *lopers*, or sliding pieces, when open. Eventually, with the
substitution of a chest of drawers for the open stand, such pieces
developed into the bureau typical of the eighteenth century. Though the
arrangement was by no means invariable, bureaux made before about
1740 tend to have a storage compartment, or *well*, in the space between
the lopers which is reached via a sliding panel in the floor of the desk
section. Further storage could be obtained by mounting a bookcase or
cabinet on the level top surface above the fall.

*An oak bureau from the
Lancashire/Cheshire
region, 1775-1810.
Typical of (though by no
means exclusive to) case
furniture from this region
are the quarter-columns
inset on the corners, the
common use of mahogany
crossbanding and par-
quetry banding, used here
on the plinths of the
quarter-columns.*

A hanging food cupboard of the mid seventeenth century. The IHS monogram inscribed on the top rail suggests that this oak example was used in a church for storing dole.

This early eighteenth-century pine cupboard originally furnished the birthplace of William Cobbett, the nineteenth-century reformer, at Farnham, Surrey. Owing to its lowly status and its susceptibility to woodworm, relatively little pine furniture of this period has survived.

CUPBOARDS

Terms such as 'cupboard', 'dresser' (or 'dressing board') and 'sideboard' share common etymological roots and in earlier times were occasionally interchangeable, being more descriptive of function than of any specific constructional form. Originally the word *cupboard* implied simply a board, or side table, which held and displayed cups or other plate. During the seventeenth century the term was increasingly applied to forms of furniture enclosed by doors and the earlier connotation was gradually abandoned. To avoid ambiguity, all terms appearing in this book are used in their modern sense.

Perishable food not stored in larders or pantries was kept in lidded hutches or in varying forms of enclosed wooden cupboard, normally pierced in some way for ventilation. Many of the cupboards surviving from the early sixteenth century tend to be of boarded construction with pierced openings in a variety of traceried designs based on the Gothic architectural style. Most of the extant examples appear to have been intended to be freestanding, although many have now lost their bases. A greater profusion of both boarded and joined food cupboards has survived from the seventeenth century; in order to protect their contents from vermin, many of these were designed to hang on the wall and occasionally were even suspended from the ceiling by means of ropes and pulleys. Ventilation of joined examples was effected by constructing the doors to frame a series of turned spindles or by providing panels of perforated wood or tin. The comparatively high quality of some surviving examples implies the status of ceremonial use and it seems likely that these were often associated with either the domestic ritual of livery, the nightly distribution of food and candles to members of the household, or the public custom of dole, the charitable dispensation of provisions to the parish poor.

In some districts it was common to build cupboards intended for dry foodstuffs, such as salt or spices, into the fabric of the fireplace or chimney to preserve their contents from damp. A similar consideration influenced the siting of portable spice cupboards, containing a series of small drawers behind a single door; these were kept near the hearth both for warmth and for convenience when cooking.

Dining has always played an important part in the rituals of everyday life and in former times was often a complex and formal event. The plate or crockery pertaining to it were as costly as the householder could afford

'Don't Touch' by John Mallard Bromley, exhibited 1880. The simple furnishings of this English or Welsh cottage interior include a cricket table (used here for rolling pastry on), a wedged stool and a boarded cradle with an arched hood. A fixed settle flanks the fireplace.

An oak chest of drawers from an old house in Farnham, Surrey, first half of the eighteenth century. The half-round mouldings applied to the members framing the drawers imitate oriental design.

A pine chest of drawers painted to simulate satinwood and mahogany, probably from the north Midlands, early twentieth century. The splash-board top indicates that it doubled as a dressing table or washstand.

A boarded oak chest, mid seventeenth century. The manner in which the saw-cuts forming the legs are continued higher on to the external surface of the end boards is a West Country characteristic.

An oak press cupboard from the Pennines. The frieze is carved with the owner's initials and the date 1695.

and, when not in use, were stored on or in a suitably prestigious piece of furniture. During the seventeenth century this piece was frequently a *press cupboard*, a large cupboard with a recessed upper section which was normally flanked by a pair of turned pillars, though on later examples these tend to have been reduced to a pair of vestigial pendants. Press cupboards were given pride of place in a hall or parlour and their high status is indicated by the frequent inclusion of initials and dates in their carved decoration. In some parts of England (notably the Lake District) press cupboards were often built in as partitions between rooms and occasionally have separate compartments, the front ones opening into the main parlour and others accessible only from the adjoining room. Although the occasional boarded example has been recorded, most press cupboards are of joined and panelled construction.

Space was always at a premium in the smaller cottage or farmhouse;

Right: This mid eighteenth-century corner cupboard from a farmhouse in Lincolnshire makes good use of burr elm (taken from a growth on the surface of the tree) for the fielded panels and drawer fronts.

Below: A pine corner cupboard from Yorkshire, c.1800. The fielded panels are neatly chamfered internally as well as on the exterior, the shelves are shaped and there is an internal arch. Such cupboards were located in a primary downstairs room and used to store and display china and glass.

corner cupboards, either full-height or wall-hanging, made the most of otherwise unused areas and became popular from the early eighteenth century onwards. In 1833 John Claudius Loudon, the author of a pioneer study of homes and furniture for the working classes, advocated the use of corner cupboards as an accessory to a dresser, for keeping 'cups and saucers, glasses, the tea-caddy, liquors in daily use, &c.' and recommended them as supplying 'a handsome article of furniture' at little cost. Glazed upper sections were favoured as they were well-suited to displaying a prized dinner service arranged on the shelves. Since glazing

An oak writing cabinet, or scrutoire, mounted on a chest of drawers, early eighteenth century. This was the precursor of the drop-front secretaire and formed an alternative to slope-fronted bureaux.

An oak press cupboard from Westmorland. The frieze is carved with the three initials (two forenames and shared surname) of a married couple, arranged in a standard triangular format, and the date 1684.

An oak house-keeping cupboard from the north-west, probably early nineteenth century. Such pieces are closely related to the 'formal' high dresser used in grander households and, when used primarily for storing china, fulfilled much the same function. The square reeded columns on the corners of the lower section of this example are a feature associated with Cheshire. Mahogany veneers and cross-banding are liberally used for decorative effect.

A pine housekeeping cupboard found in Lincolnshire, mid nineteenth-century.

An early example of a pine low dresser, early eighteenth-century. This fully enclosed dresser was discovered serving as a shop counter in Westhampnett, West Sussex. Mouldings have been applied to the three drawers at the top to give the double-fronted appearance that was popular at this period.

tended to be more expensive, however, many cupboards with solid wooden doors solved the problem of display by having narrow double doors which could be deliberately left open without getting in the way. The doors were neatly finished on their inner surfaces and the front edges of the shelves were normally shaped in an attractive manner. Small drawers were occasionally included for additional storage.

While it formed part of the furnishings of a grand house rather than those of the ordinary cottage, the *housekeeping cupboard* deserves a brief mention here, if only because it was primarily used, even though not owned, by the servants. Housekeeping cupboards were generally large and imposing pieces of storage furniture which combined a base made up mainly of drawers with an upper section of shelves enclosed by doors. They contained the household linen, the best china and glass, and often some of the more valuable grocery items, such as tea and coffee. All these things were under the direct supervision of the housekeeper and the cupboard — or a series of them in a particularly large house — stood under lock and key in her quarters or, more rarely, in a hall or upstairs landing.

An oak low dresser from the Lancashire/Cheshire/west Yorkshire region, late eighteenth century.

An oak low dresser, 1760-1800. The imitation quoins decorating the corners suggest a south Lancashire origin, probably in the Liverpool area.

A painted pine high dresser from north-western England, possibly Cheshire, early nineteenth century.

DRESSERS

The natural desire for display was a prime factor in the development of the dresser. The utilitarian kitchen dresser is largely derived from the functional *dressing board* of the middle ages, a basic surface on which food was prepared. However, the all-important ritual of dining in early times also called for a finer 'hall' version of the dresser on which meals could be finally dressed and suitably displayed before serving. During the seventeenth century this function was performed by any suitable piece of furniture — large side tables and court cupboards (open-shelved structures). A related piece was the press cupboard (discussed in the previous chapter) which, in addition to providing storage for dining articles, also allowed a small measure of display. To some extent, these may be regarded as descendants of the medieval *dressoir* or *buffet*, a grand piece of furniture often having a high back or canopy and sometimes several tiers (their number dictated by the social status of the owner).

An elm high dresser from the Quantock/ Sedgemoor area of Somerset, c.1800. This variety with slab ends appears to have been peculiar to this region.

An oak high dresser found in Dorset but possibly of Devon origin. The shaped frieze and apron, the turned legs and the original wooden knobs indicate a date range of 1820-50.

By the end of the seventeenth century both the court cupboard and the press cupboard had become unfashionable over much of England and specialised dressers or sideboards were increasingly taking their place. Early extant examples of these tend to be of *low dresser* type (without a superstructure of shelves) and take the form of long side tables with drawers or are fully enclosed with a combination of drawers and cupboards. While it must have been a common practice to mount a set of shelves on the wall above such dressers, the true *high dresser*, permanently fitted with a shelved superstructure, does not appear to have come into widespread use in England until the eighteenth century. (This observation refers only to 'formal' dressers used in reception rooms; it is quite possible that the utilitarian dressers located in kitchens were commonly fitted with shelved superstructures at a much earlier date.)

Influenced by local economic and traditional factors, the status accorded the dresser varied enormously from one region to another and

An oak high dresser, 1750-90, from a house in the Lake District.

A beech and oak trestle table, seventeenth or eighteenth century.

An oak side table of lowboy form, 1740-80.

An oak high dresser of a type associated with the west Midlands, 1790-1820. Note the characteristically late use of cabriole legs in the north of England.

this had a direct effect on constructional methods, decorative techniques, timber and form. Dressers were described by an eighteenth-century joiner living in Sussex as being made of deal and this probably reflects their comparatively low status in the south-east at that period. Similarly, eighteenth-century dressers from other regions with agriculturally based economies, such as East Anglia and the West Country, are seldom of exceptional merit. The Quantocks and Sedgemoor area of Somerset produced a distinctive variety, usually of elm or pine and having a somewhat crude slab-ended form of construction. The industrial north, by contrast, produced several types of very fine dresser, those from parts

of the north-west and the west Midlands tending to be open-based with
an overlapping chronological sequence of turned, cabriole and straight,
square-section legs. Superior oak was commonly used and decorative
treatments frequently included mahogany crossbanding and fine inlays.
A superstructure of shelves, if present, was generally provided with a
cupboard at each end. Dressers found in other areas of the north, notably
in parts of Lancashire, Yorkshire and the Lake District, were normally
made with their bases fully enclosed as drawers and cupboards. Oak was
a normal material and the superstructures were frequently embellished
with impressive fluted pilasters.

*An oak high dresser, probably from north Yorkshire, 1750-90. A full-height
cupboard door, flanked by banks of drawers, is typical of the bases of dressers from
this region.*

A late nineteenth-century pine dresser having a base entirely devoted to drawers and decorated with large split turnings to both upper and lower sections. The type is associated with Cornwall and west Devon. Glazed doors were a nineteenth-century innovation.

A form of low dresser typical of the Lancashire/Cheshire region; late eighteenth-century. The top lifts as a lid to a chest-like storage compartment behind three false drawer fronts; the lower six drawers are real. The oak carcase is decorated with mahogany veneers and crossbanding.

The growing wealth, or pretensions to it, of many in the lower classes during the nineteenth century gave rise to an increased formality in interior decor; the status of the dresser declined and by the end of the century it was more likely to be relegated purely to kitchen use. The front room of the house was very often set aside as a formal 'parlour', in imitation of the drawing-rooms of grand mansions; a traditional dresser was considered inappropriate in such an environment and its place was taken by one of the finer sideboards which were becoming readily available from factories.

A pine trestle table; nineteenth-century.

An oak 'long table'; late eighteenth-century. The top of this example is fixed and consists of three planks linked at each end by cross-members, or end cleats.

TABLES

The large dining tables dating from before 1800 and normally found in larger dwellings such as farmhouses reflect the earlier social custom of a time when the family dined communally with house servants and farmworkers. The dining table of the medieval hall-house typically consisted of a board or boards (the 'table' itself, before the word was extended to include supports) which rested on two or more separate trestles. Trestle tables have continued to be produced up to the present day but, as their fashionable use for formal dining began to be superseded by more prestigious tables with joined frames after the mid sixteenth century, they were gradually demoted to more utilitarian roles and a large proportion of examples surviving from the nineteenth century were originally provided by breweries for pubs and taverns. Trestle tables are notoriously difficult to date accurately and a great many are probably much later than they may at first appear. Nail types and the marks of sawing techniques may provide some indication of date. If originally owned by a brewery, its name or initials may be stamped or stencilled under the top and these can occasionally be traced and identified.

In large dining tables of joined construction made during the seventeenth and early eighteenth centuries the top is fixed to a frame having four or more legs which are tied by stretchers and normally turned. The number of legs was determined by the length of the table; four or six legs were usual on most tables (typically 7 or 8 feet, 2.1 to 2.4 metres, long), although exceptionally long tables used in grander houses could be provided with as many as twenty. Very often such tables bear carved decoration on only one side as it was a common practice to stand them near a wall, served on the plain wall side by a fixed bench and on the facing side by a form which left the decoration exposed. As the eighteenth century progressed, tables of this type increasingly became severely functional, with simple square-section legs, frequently tapered after 1780, and a complete absence of carving.

The dual purpose of these later tables for both dining and kitchen use demanded versatility. In Devon it was common for the top not to be fixed; one side was kept scrubbed for kitchen duty but reversed to show the polished side when used for meals. The problem of dual purpose was solved in a different way for the Victorian descendant — the ubiquitous pine kitchen table; the fixed top was scrubbed but, since the frame and legs were properly stained and varnished, the table easily converted to an attractive dining surface by simply covering it with a tablecloth.

Alternatively, the top was kept polished and a *table board*, a separate flat wooden cover, was placed on it as protection when preparing food.

The advantages of a table which occupied little space when not in use yet which could be considerably enlarged when desired, by means of folding leaves hinged to the fixed top, were recognised in the sixteenth century. By the mid seventeenth century the principle had evolved into what is now known as a *gateleg table* (a contemporary term was *oval* table), in which the leaves are supported in the horizontal position by joined open structures (looking much like gates — hence the name) which fold back against the sides when the leaves are no longer required. The gateleg technique was used for tables in a wide range of sizes, from those with swivel tops that folded completely flat, more conventional small versions for occasional use and some with only a single leaf, to very large dining tables provided with four gates — two each side — a few of which were capable of accommodating sixteen or more people.

The tops of early gateleg tables are normally fixed to the frame by means of pegs or nails inserted from above; the joints between the top and the folding leaves are generally either the flush *butt* type or the *tongue-and-groove* variety, in which a continuous tongue running along the inside edge of each leaf fits into a corresponding groove on the edge of the table-top when the leaf is raised. By 1720 it was becoming common for the top to be secured by screws inserted through gouges in the rails from below. The joints between top and leaves were now frequently the *rule joint* type, in which a convex moulded edge on the top fits a concave moulded edge on the leaf.

The oriental trend which began to dominate furniture design during the late Stuart period eventually had a profound effect not only on the opulent products of high fashion but on more vernacular pieces as well. Cabriole legs (and related straight forms, of round section with pad feet) are not ideally suited to a stretcher framework and their gradual adoption for drop-leaf tables during the first half of the eighteenth century rendered the gateleg system obsolete. Instead, a *swing-leg* system was devised in which the tops of two of the legs (at opposite corners) are joined to rails which pivot on a wooden hinge (or *knuckle joint*) at the centre of each underframe side so that the legs could be swung out to support the leaves when desired. The same method was retained for succeeding leg styles: the straight square-section (*Marlborough*) leg of the mid eighteenth century onwards, the tapered square-section leg after about 1770, and the turned leg of the nineteenth century.

An oak gateleg table, 1680-1730. The rebates in the gate legs and the side stretchers, which allow the gates to fold flat when not in use, can be clearly seen.

Another form of leaf suspension was better suited to tables of a smaller size. The *Pembroke* style of drop-leaf table was introduced in the second half of the eighteenth century and in this type two fairly narrow leaves are simply supported in the upright position by wooden brackets hinged to the underframe. One or two drawers are frequently incorporated at one end and, typically, there is a matching mock drawer face at the other end for the sake of symmetry. While such tables were initially intended for richer homes, their small dimensions were soon seen as perfectly suited to the limited space of humbler houses and a range of more modest variations developed, including robust pine examples designed for kitchen use.

Tables having only three legs provided stability on the uneven floors common in less affluent houses and may be broadly divided into two categories. The first type consists of a circular top supported by three (or occasionally four) splayed legs and is popularly known as a *cricket table*. Despite a common myth, the name has no connection with the sport but is derived from an old term for stools. Since the archetypal stool (or *cricket*) has a circular top and three legs, a table of essentially the same form has acquired the same name. Such tables are normally either of wedged construction, in which a rough slab top has the legs wedged into it, or of joined construction, whereby the legs are joined at their tops by

Left: A small oak table of Pembroke form, 1820-50. The mahogany crossbanding on the drawer front is inset from the edge — a feature typical of northern furniture. This drawer front is false; the real drawer is at the other end.

Right: A pine and fruitwood cricket table found in Nottinghamshire, 1770-1820. The original paint finish is a dark over pale brown scumble. Note the pad feet.

a triangular underframe and, very often, lower down by stretchers. They were frequently referred to as *drinking tables* in Georgian times ('cricket table' is a relatively modern term) and were widely used in alehouses. In the home they served as centre tables for casual meals and other everyday household use. Their usefulness was occasionally increased by fitting a shelf on the stretchers or by the thoughtful inclusion of a drawer or cupboard. The earliest extant examples appear to be no earlier than the seventeenth century, although wedged types do appear in medieval illustrations.

The second category of three-legged table is the *pedestal* variety, having the legs dovetailed into the base of a central pillar. Tops are normally circular but are also found in other shapes, including rectangular and octagonal. Such tripod tables were made in the seventeenth century but did not become common until the beginning of the Georgian period. They remained highly fashionable for more than a century; small versions served as candlestands or for occasional use and larger tables were suited to the genteel vogue for taking hot drinks such as tea, coffee and chocolate. In many examples the top can be made to tilt to a vertical position; the table thus takes up less space when not in use. This aspect no doubt enhanced their desirability in the eyes of those living in more cramped accommodation and by the end of the eighteenth century the

A tripod pedestal table made from yew, a relatively expensive timber, 1810-50. The top can be made to tilt to a vertical position. The attenuated cabriole legs are a nineteenth-century form and identical to those on many similar North American tables of this period. Tables with legs of this type are too often erroneously attributed to the mid eighteenth century by British collectors and this is an example of where a comparative analysis of datable American furniture can be of great benefit in establishing a true chronology.

An elm and ash pedestal table from Cornwall, first half of the nineteenth century. This regional type of low table is reputed to have been intended as a lampstand for lacemakers.

Left: Home-made furniture was undoubtedly common in the past, but little has survived. This example, a work table painted with miniature scenes, has been made from various scraps of wood that came to hand; the box and base are of recycled pine, the top is mahogany and an old chair leg has ingeniously been inverted to serve as the pillar. The underside of the lid is inscribed 'J. Mosley June 8th 1877'.

Right: A pine side table found in Sussex, 1770-1820. Although the straight square-section (Marlborough) legs are mounted with pegged mortise-and-tenon joints and neatly chamfered on the inner edge, the top is more crudely affixed by large hand-forged nails.

tripod pedestal table had become a familiar item of furniture in even the humbler farmhouse or cottage. A rudimentary form of pedestal table appears to have been popular in Cornwall. To avoid the expense and skill of making the conventional cabrioles dovetailed into the pedestal, the pillar is merely fixed to a slab-like platform base into which simple stake-like legs are wedged.

The making and mending of clothing and other needlework was a constant occupation in past times and tables specifically dedicated to such tasks had evolved by the late eighteenth century. Storage of materials and equipment was of prime importance and many work tables tended to be little more than a lidded box or a bank of drawers upon legs or a pedestal stand. By the second half of the nineteenth century a large lidded container on a tripod base had become popular.

Oak stools, both seventeenth-century. (Left) A boarded type made from the middle ages onwards. (Right) A joined box stool containing a partitioned storage compartment beneath the hinged seat.

Tables intended to stand against a wall are easily recognised by the fact that decoration is restricted to only three sides, with the back normally left unfinished. They fulfilled a wide variety of functions — from prestigious display pieces in reception rooms to workaday surfaces in kitchens — and some developed into specialised forms. A particularly distinctive type of side table evolved during the late seventeenth and early eighteenth centuries, in which three (occasionally more) drawers are arranged around a central arch. Such forms were obviously designed to be sat at and were probably intended primarily as dressing tables, although they also provided a convenient writing surface. They are commonly known as *lowboys*; the term is relatively modern, however, and appears to be derived merely from their frequent resemblance to the bases of chests on stands (referred to in the United States, whence the term 'lowboy' originally came, as 'highboys'). The two types of furniture are related, however, and were occasionally made as a matching set.

An oak chair, south Yorkshire/north Derbyshire type, second half of the seventeenth century. The pair of crescent-shaped slats and the scrolled finials are distinctive regional characteristics.

An oak armchair with caned back panel, late seventeenth/early eighteenth century. An early paint finish of brown over yellow scumble survives.

SEATING

Stools provided the usual seating in less affluent homes until well into Stuart times and still remained essential and commonplace long after chairs had begun to replace them for dining use after the mid seventeenth century. Forms (backless benches) are basically no more than elongated stools for the use of more than one person and may generally be considered within much the same context. Stools of wedged, turned or boarded construction were made in nearly all periods and those of joined construction from the mid sixteenth century onwards. Functions ranged from casual seating to work use; high stools served for office or factory and low stools for occupations such as blacksmithing, milking or other menial work. Low stools were referred to as *crickets* and were ideally suited for seating near the hearth (hence the title of Dickens's story *The Cricket on the Hearth*), their diminutive height allowing the occupant to escape the worst of the smoke billowing from the inefficient fireplaces usual before the late nineteenth century.

Chairs in general, and those provided with arms in particular, have long been traditionally considered as a symbol of rank. The old courtly convention in which only the leader (still called the 'chairman') and perhaps one or two honoured guests were seated on armchairs was echoed even in relatively humble households. The head of the family, and possibly his wife, might sit upon chairs at the dining table while the children and other lesser members of the household either sat on stools and forms or simply stood. Evidence refutes the widely held belief that *single* chairs (that is, those without arms) did not evolve until the early seventeenth century. Such chairs were known as *backstools* (literally a stool with a backrest) in early times and the concept is elementary. They were certainly known in the classical world and are mentioned in English documentary sources as early as the first half of the fifteenth century.

The vernacular chair exhibits enormous variations in terms of form, style and construction and tends to be one of the most distinctive and significant expressions of regional traditions. Its special importance in these respects is reflected in the length of the following discussion. The majority of examples may be broadly divided into three classifications according to their method of construction — joined, turned and wedged (including Windsor types) — and for our purposes the categories are best considered separately.

Joined chairs

The armchair typical of the Stuart period tends to be an imposing but

An oak slat-back chair from northern England, c.1720. Note the disproportionately high back typical of chairs of this period.

unyielding affair, with a panelled back and solid seat. Padding was generally provided by separate cushions or by the bulky clothing of the occupant. Fixed upholstery was normally restricted to the more affluent, although chairs upholstered in leather (the so-called *Cromwellian* type) became increasingly popular in the southern counties. In contrast to the relative plainness of many chairs found in the south of England during the seventeenth and early eighteenth centuries, a large number of those made in the north and the north Midlands bear a great deal of ornamentation, both carved and applied, and often possess distinctive regional characteristics. Perhaps the best-known of these characteristics are the pair of crescent-shaped slats occurring on chairs from south Yorkshire and north Derbyshire and the pyramidal finials on those from Lancashire and Cheshire. Other regional traits associated with south Yorkshire/north Derbyshire chairs are the arcaded form of back and pairs of scrolled finials.

Joined single chairs from the first half of the seventeenth century tend to have fairly high seats and the front stretcher is always placed at a low level, in the same position as those on armchairs. After 1650 the seat height was generally reduced as the chairs were more commonly made in sets for dining at gateleg tables and the front stretcher was typically (though by no means invariably, as has sometimes been asserted) positioned higher, on the same level as the two highest side stretchers.

The fashion for more lightly constructed chairs with caned seats and caned backs, which was introduced from the continent shortly after 1660, was gradually translated into a vernacular form. Instead of a caned seat, ordinary chairs often retained the traditional type of solid wood and a framed panel or a series of vertical slats was frequently substituted for a caned back. Chairs of this kind made during the final decade of the seventeenth century and the beginning of the eighteenth century also tended to reflect the vogue for disproportionately high backs which had developed after 1680.

In the first half of the eighteenth century the vernacular joined chair began to assimilate the more salient elements of the oriental style which were prevalent at that time. In their translation to a 'peasant' culture, however, such characteristics frequently suffered a less than scholastic interpretation and were often combined with more traditional European features in a somewhat naive and hybrid manner. The solid vasiform splat of oriental inspiration, for instance, was typically united with a conventional base having turned legs and stretchers. Oriental cabriole legs were adopted for better chairs and, by mid century, were supplemented by the alternative Marlborough leg (also of oriental origin), which was square in section and normally chamfered on the inner edge. By this time too, it was becoming common to pierce the splat in a variety of patterns and to extend the crest rail beyond the uprights into rococo flourishes or *ears*, in the Chippendale manner. Indeed, the influence of the styles associated with Thomas Chippendale is so apparent in even these humble chairs, normally of oak, elm or fruitwood and with solid wooden seats, that they are popularly known as 'country Chippendale '.

The combined neo-classical/French rococo style, typified by the designs of George Hepplewhite, exerted a similar influence in the last decades of the eighteenth century. Vernacular chairs in this style are generally characterised by a humped crest rail combined with a waisted splat and, very often, square-section front legs tapered on their inner faces. Such chairs are colloquially referred to as *camelbacks*, from the distinctive shape of the crest rail, or, predictably, as 'country Hepplewhite'.

Chairs conforming to a style prevalent at the very end of the eighteenth century and in the first half of the nineteenth are similarly named after the designer whose patterns exemplified the type — Thomas Sheraton.

An elm 'corner' chair, 1770-1820: a type of chair primarily intended for office or tavern use. Contemporary domestic inventories indicate that it was frequently used in conjunction with a desk. This example has a removable rush seat.

Left: An elm chair from East Anglia, 1800-40. A low square-back style. The concave wooden seat is a regional feature.

Right: This elm chair of c.1810 exhibits the combination of influences on its 'Hepplewhite' prototype. The tapering of the front legs is purely neo-classical. The humped crest rail and curved uprights, however, are derived from a 'shield-back' design which was influenced by the French rococo style.

These, the so-called 'country Sheraton' variety, are essentially character-ised by a low square back. As the Grecian style, an offshoot of the neo-classical, increasingly dominated furniture fashion after 1800, the hori-zontal aspects were accentuated and the central rail of the back was sometimes given extra prominence and carved with classically inspired motifs. Very often the crest rail was made flat and broad, occasionally overlapping the uprights, and turned legs began to be substituted for the square-section variety. Arms might be terminated in highly pronounced vertical scrolls. The virtual demise of the joined solid-seat chair over most of England in the latter part of the nineteenth century may be explained by the ever more accessible upholstered mahogany pieces for parlour use, caned chairs for bedrooms and the eventual supremacy of turned and Windsor types for the kitchen.

One of the most distinctive regional forms of armchair produced during the eighteenth and nineteenth centuries was the so-called *lambing chair* of the Lancashire and Yorkshire Dales. These are distinguished particularly by their prominent wings flanking the back and they are frequently provided with a cupboard or drawer mounted below the seat. Despite their popular name, it is unlikely that they have any specific connection with lambing and they were probably intended merely as comfortable hearthside armchairs.

Turned chairs

Joined chairs were frequently embellished with turned decoration from the sixteenth century onwards, but chairs made almost *wholly* (with the exception of seats and the occasional square-section member) by the use of the turner's lathe form an older and unmistakably distinct group. The turned chair is of ancient origin; extant examples in Scandinavia date from before 1300 and similar pieces were probably common in medieval England. The earliest English survival appears to be the so-called 'King Stephen's Throne' in Hereford Cathedral but dating it precisely has proved difficult and dates ranging from the twelfth to the sixteenth century have been suggested by various authorities.

We are concerned here, however, primarily with the turned chair of the eighteenth and nineteenth centuries, by which time it had become

Left: An oak armchair dated 1691. The style of the carving suggests an origin in the Yorkshire Dales near Leeds. A side door gives access to a compartment under the seat.
Right: A winged oak armchair, Lancashire/Yorkshire Dales, eighteenth century. This example is evidently related to the 1691 armchair from the Leeds area. Here the seat is strung with rope webbing to support a cushion and the base compartment is fitted with a drawer. The pyramidal finials are a form associated with Lancashire.

(Left) An ash and birch bow-back Windsor chair from the West Country, c.1800. (Right) An elm dug-out chair from the north-west, late eighteenth or early nineteenth century.

Opposite: A winged armchair in pine, elm and sycamore from the Lancashire/ Yorkshire Dales area, early nineteenth century.

An ash spindleback chair with elm seat, second half of the nineteenth century. The rear uprights are stamped with the initials of Philip Clissett of Bosbury, Herefordshire.

established as the common type in cottages, farmhouses and smaller urban homes in nearly all parts of England. While the back designs of some examples emulate the fashionable characteristics of superior joined chairs, the large majority of turned chairs may be broadly divided into two classifications: the *spindleback*, in which the back consists of various arrangements of turned spindles, and the *ladderback*, which has a series of horizontal slats, usually bowed for comfort. With the exception of those made in the west Midlands, the seats of all kinds were typically made from rushes, a readily available material which provided some comfort but was also cheap to replace when it inevitably wore out.

Although rush seats are fairly common in west Midlands chairs, a large proportion of examples have a wooden panel held in grooves on the seat rails, normally fronted by a wooden frieze, and this seating method is a distinctive regional feature. A variety of both ladderback and spindleback types was produced, those made in the counties of Shropshire and Staffordshire being frequently distinguished by a curved wooden rail, or *bar*, across the tops of the rear uprights. Turned chairs from several regions are occasionally stamped with the name or initials of the maker. Perhaps the best-known west Midlands stamps are those of the Kerry family, working in Evesham, Worcestershire, during the second quarter of the nineteenth century, and the initials of Philip Clissett (1817-1913) of Bosbury, Herefordshire. Other initials found include those of Clissett's brother-in-law, William Cole, and John Warander, father and son of the same name, working in Bransford, Worcestershire. Clissett was to achieve a measure of fame during the final decades of his long life due to his association with the Arts and Crafts movement, which was then becoming fashionable. He was admired by Ernest Gimson, one of the founders of the Cotswold School, and his chair designs were the inspiration for some of Gimson's products.

Perhaps the most familiar (and most constantly reproduced) designs of turned chair are those of the north-western counties of Lancashire and Cheshire. In common with those of some other northern regions, the Lancashire/Cheshire chairs are typified by front legs of round section, tapered and terminating in pad feet. There are three major varieties of spindlebacks in this region. The first two are characterised by a distinctive flattened crest rail having a pair of pointed projections on its upper edge. Like the front legs, these projections are a simplification of features found on fashionable joined chairs of the eighteenth century. In the first variety (the most numerous) the crest rail is curved and fixed between turned uprights. In the second type the crest rail surmounts square-section uprights and flourishes into the rococo ears of the Chippendale style. The third major variety of spindleback found in Lancashire and Cheshire is primarily distinguished by a shell motif carved in the centre of the crest rail and, typically, the lower back rails swell at the points where they receive the spindles. This type has long been known as a

Three turned ash chairs from the Lancashire/Cheshire region, 1780-1850. (Left) Standard double-row spindleback. (Centre) Wavy-line ladderback. (Right) Bar-top ladderback from the Billinge/Pemberton/Wigan area of south Lancashire.

Three turned chairs from the Lancashire/Cheshire region, 1800-50. (Left) A 'crested' spindleback. (Centre) A ladderback of Billinge type. (Right) An eared spindleback.

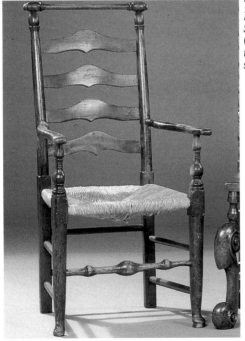

An ash ladderback armchair of Macclesfield type, Cheshire/Lancashire, mid nineteenth century. The distinctive turned bar across the rear uprights could be used to support a rug or cloth draped over the back of the chair to make it more comfortable.

(Left) A yew and elm bow-back Windsor from north-eastern England, c.1850. (Centre) A yew and elm bow-back Windsor from the Thames valley, c.1790. (Right) An ash and elm bow-back Windsor from the West Country, still bearing its original dark green paint, c.1800.

An ash ladderback chair from Lincolnshire, first half of the nineteenth century. The square-section cabriole legs are a distinctive regional characteristic.

Left: An ash and birch spindleback of Liverpool type, Lancashire/Cheshire, 1790-1840. The shell motif in the crest rail is a distinctive feature.
Right: An ash ladderback armchair of Billinge type made in the Billinge/Pemberton/Wigan area of south Lancashire, c.1830.

Liverpool chair and was so described in a Gillow's cost book of 1801, but it was made in several other parts of the north-west region as well. Several examples bear the stamp of members of the Leicester family, who worked in Macclesfield, Cheshire, during the early to mid nineteenth century.

The enormous variety of ladderback chairs made in the Lancashire/ Cheshire area includes the so-called *wavy line* pattern, in which the slats undulate at each end, and those having a bar across the rear uprights. One type, associated with the Billinge area, has a scrolled crest rail between two large turned finials mounted on the rear uprights. A variant which may have originated in Macclesfield has a distinctive turned bar terminating in reel-like shapes.

Less sophisticated designs were favoured further north, in the rural dales of Lancashire, Yorkshire and Cumbria. Both ladderbacks and spindlebacks were produced, the latter being characterised by only one row of spindles. The wide range of plain and bar-top ladderback chairs made in Lincolnshire shows several regional features. The most immediately obvious idiosyncrasy is possibly the frequent use of square-section cabrioles, surmounted by turnings, for the front legs. These are associated with a chairmaking industry in Spilsby, Alford and Louth.

Wedged (Windsor) chairs

Furniture of wedged construction was, for the most part, devoid of decoration and confined to a workaday environment but around 1700, or shortly after, the technique was adapted and refined by professional craftsmen as the basic element of a design classic — the *Windsor chair* — that was to revolutionise seating over the next three centuries. The earliest examples appear to have been produced in the Thames valley area and probably took their name from the local market town of Windsor, Berkshire, an ideal distribution centre for the region. Windsor is situated on the Thames, a convenient location at a time when goods were most easily transported to London (the prime retail target) by river. 'Windsor' has since become accepted as the generic term for any chair in which both the legs and the uprights are wedged into holes bored in a slab seat.

The central portions of the backs of eighteenth-century Windsor chairs are generally composed either entirely of vertical spindles or of a combination of central splat (often vasiform and occasionally pierced) and

Left: A bow-back Windsor armchair from the Thames valley, yew with an elm seat, 1780-1810. The cabriole legs at the front are linked by a bowed front stretcher. A similar chair bears the trade label of William Webb of Newington, Surrey.

Right: A Windsor armchair in the scroll-back style, Buckinghamshire/Oxfordshire, nineteenth century.

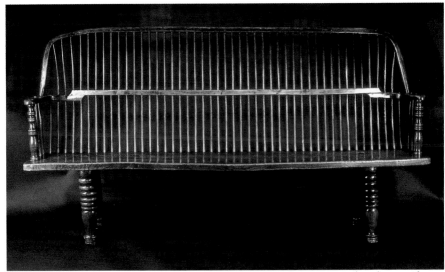

An elm and beech Windsor settee from the West Country, early nineteenth century.

A painted pine washstand, first half of the nineteenth century. The top surface is painted to simulate marble.

A pine linen press painted to simulate curly maple, found in Sussex, second half of the nineteenth century. The upper section is fitted with a set of sliding trays.

flanking spindles. In the earliest type, the *comb-back*, these members are united at the top by a horizontal crest rail, the ends of which frequently flourish into rounded ears. An alternative type, the *bow-back*, had developed by mid century and here the crest rail was replaced by a bent hoop, the ends of which terminated in either the arm bow or the seat. In the middle of the eighteenth century also a bowed front stretcher was introduced as an optional form and cabriole front legs were occasionally being used on better chairs. Windsor styles diversified still further during the nineteenth century. The most striking innovation was the *scroll-back*, a combination of the standard back form of joined chairs in the Grecian style — scrolled and round-fronted rear uprights linked by a plain crest rail and a plain or decorative lower rail — with a conventional Windsor base.

As long ago as 1725 Daniel Defoe remarked on the 'vast quantity of beechwood' growing in Buckinghamshire and its use by local chairmakers. During the nineteenth century the Windsor chair industry of that county, centred particularly in High Wycombe, grew to serve the south Midlands and much of East Anglia and southern England. A contributory factor in its phenomenal growth must have been the proximity of the enormous London market. There were nearly one hundred chair factories in High Wycombe alone by 1877 and they were producing an estimated 4700 chairs a day. Most workers were employed on a piecework basis, paid per component or skill provided, and many lived as outworkers, performing such tasks as turning legs and stretchers in the countryside and then delivering their finished parts to the factory. Apart from beech, ash, elm and fruitwood were readily available. Elm was favoured for seats since it can be bored easily without causing it to split.

Several makers extended the Buckinghamshire tradition into neighbouring counties and some are well-known from the maker's stamps appearing on their products. Among these are the Prior family of Uxbridge, Middlesex, a distinguished dynasty of chairmakers recorded from the mid eighteenth to the mid nineteenth century and particularly associated with a bow-back design incorporating three pierced splats. Other regional makers include the two Stephen Hazells, father and son, who worked in Oxford during the nineteenth century and whose most typical Windsor style was the scroll-back.

A Windsor chair industry also arose in the West Country during the eighteenth and nineteenth centuries and some of the most distinctive products are a range of chair designs made in and around the village of

Left: A bow-back Windsor chair from Buckinghamshire, ash with elm seat, first half of the nineteenth century. The back, with a wheel motif in the splat, is given additional support by two bracing spindles secured to a 'bobtail', a rear extension of the seat.

Right: A bow-back Windsor chair from Buckinghamshire, mid nineteenth century. A Gothic tracery design.

Yealmpton in Devon from the early 1800s up to about 1850. These include bow-back armchairs in which the arms are bent from flattened sections of ash and those in which both the back-bow and the arms are formed from one continuous member, a style formerly thought to have been peculiar to North America.

Another Windsor type whose manufacture appears to have been confined to the vicinity of only one village is a square-back design of neoclassical influence made at Mendlesham, Suffolk, in the first half of the nineteenth century. Typically, these have a pierced splat flanked by spindles and a row of three turned balls below the top rail. Since they were regarded as special rather than everyday chairs, they are nearly always of armchair form. Oral tradition attributes their invention to Daniel and Richard Day, father and son, but no contemporary record of a local chairmaker named Daniel Day has so far been found. A chairmaker named Richard Day, however, was born in Mendlesham in 1783 and died there in 1838. The chairs are something of an enigma since they appear to represent an entirely isolated tradition of Windsor chairmaking in East Anglia.

By contrast, the Windsor chair industries of north-eastern England were diverse and extremely extensive. Manufacturing centres existed in all counties — from Leicestershire in the south of this region to Northumberland in the north — and a wide repertoire of styles was produced. Chairs were quite often stamped with the name of the maker and, sometimes, also that of the town in which he worked. Among the

A painted pine spoon rack, probably early nineteenth century.

An oak dough bin from northern England, possibly Yorkshire, dated 1703.

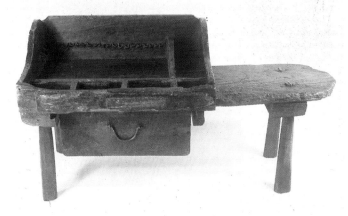

A pine and ash cobbler's bench found in Shropshire, first half of the nineteenth century. This example typically combines wedged and boarded construction.

Lincolnshire names encountered are those of John Amos of Grantham and Thomas and James Marsh of Sleaford. Nottinghamshire makers include John Gabbitass of Worksop (business continued by his widow, Elizabeth, and his younger brother, Henry, from 1839) and the Allsop family, also of Worksop, and William Wheatland, Frederick Walker and George Nicholson of Rockley. Most of these makers are recorded as working during the early to mid nineteenth century.

Two notable Windsor-chair styles, which appear to have been peculiar to the north-east, should be mentioned here. One style is a nineteenth-century variety of the comb-back, in which the broad, square-ended crest rail is supported by a series of plain spindles (and, occasionally, a central pierced splat) flanked by turned uprights. The second style may well have been invented by John Shadford, a chairmaker working in Caistor, Lincolnshire, during the Victorian period and whose workshop notebook has survived. The most distinctive design recorded in his notebook has a tall back with two rows of ornately turned spindles flanked by turned uprights and surmounted by a broad crest rail shaped on its lower edge. The type is typically fitted with rockers and is commonly known as the *Caistor chair*.

Left: A continuous-arm Windsor chair, ash with elm seat, probably made in the Yealmpton area of Devon, first half of the nineteenth century. The turned members are fashioned to resemble bamboo, with black-painted accents. Despite the chair having a superficially American appearance, the choice of timber is typically English.
Right: A highly distinctive style of Windsor chair made in the Mendlesham area of Suffolk. Fruitwood with elm seat, first half of the nineteenth century.

Two bow-back Windsor armchairs, both made from yew with elm seats. (Left) Nottinghamshire/north-east, 1840-80. (Right) Nottinghamshire, 1820-50.

Settles

The earliest movable domestic settles which are still extant date from around 1500 and were a natural development of the fixed benches ranged along walls since Saxon times. Long joined settles with relatively low, panelled backs were particularly popular in Cheshire and parts of southern Lancashire and Yorkshire from the seventeenth to the early nineteenth century. Earlier examples of these are occasionally fitted with chest-like bases, accessible by raising lids in the seat, although the majority appear to be open-based and the seats are typically strung with rope webbing to support a loose cushion. Ar-

chaic features frequently persisted for an exceptionally long time; in addition to backs having plain or fielded panels, slab arms similar to those on seventeenth-century armchairs and cabriole legs, introduced on settles in the mid eighteenth century, were still retained even after 1800.

Simpler settles of boarded construction, often with winged ends and tall matchboarded backs,

A bow-back Windsor armchair, ash with elm seat. This style is typical of those made in Lincolnshire, first half of the nineteenth century.

were made in nearly all parts of England. They were normally situated near the hearth and their semi-enclosed design provided the necessary protection from draughts. Many settles of this type (and a few grander examples of joined and panelled construction) found in the West Country incorporate a cupboard fitted with hooks in the back. Such cupboards are traditionally associated with the hanging of hams and bacon, but it seems unlikely that that was invariably their purpose and the storage of outdoor clothing presents itself as an obvious, if more mundane, alternative. The common provision of lidded compartments or drawers in the base under the seat allowed convenient storage of such fireside requisites as tools or firewood.

An elm settle from an inn at Thursley, Surrey. Precise dating of such simple furniture is difficult but the typographic style of the various inventory marks stamped on its surfaces suggests a period not later than the seventeenth or early eighteenth century. The massive slab ends have been crudely repaired at the base.

An oak joined settle dated 1708. The style of the arms and the carving on the top rail suggest an origin in south-west Yorkshire. The hinged seat allows access to a storage compartment in the base.

An oak joined settle typical of the Lancashire/Cheshire region, 1760-1820. This type is described as a 'couch chair' and analysed in precise detail in a Bolton cost book of 1802.

Left: A thirty-hour longcase clock by John Frost of Chichester, West Sussex, c.1760. The plain oak case with attached hood pillars and a straight-topped trunk door is typical of southern clocks of this period. The birdcage movement of this example is also common in this region.

Right: An eight-day longcase clock by Samuel Collier of Eccles, near Manchester, c.1785. A finer case is generally to be expected on an eight-day clock but this example is more decorative than those of its southern counterparts. Typical northern features include the freestanding hood pillars, the shaped top of the trunk door, the quarter-columns on the trunk, the canted corners on the base and the ogee bracket feet. The oak case is crossbanded and inlaid with mahogany.

LONGCASE CLOCKS

When introduced in the mid seventeenth century the longcase clock was a highly expensive luxury confined to the homes of the rich and it was not until around 1700 that simpler versions were becoming affordable to those who were less affluent. During the eighteenth century the longcase clock came to achieve a position of prestige in the ordinary house that was akin to that of the press cupboard or tester bedstead in previous times.

We are concerned here primarily with the clock as a piece of furniture rather than as a mechanical device but, since both the style and the size of the case were largely affected by the type of movement to be housed within it, a brief mention of clockwork is called for. The more expensive clocks, those which ran for eight days or more at a single winding, always had a *plate* movement, in which the wheels and pinions (gears) are mounted between a pair of vertical brass plates. Less costly clocks, running for only thirty hours and normally having plainer, smaller cases, had either a plate movement or, particularly those made in the southern counties, a *birdcage* movement, a modified version of that used in lantern clocks, in which top and bottom plates are linked by four vertical posts. The clockmaker was not responsible for making the case but it is likely to have been a local product and, since the clock dial usually bears the clockmaker's name and town (by which he can often be traced and his period of working established accurately), the case is likewise dated and set within a locality. This information conveniently provides a chronological and regional reference by which other types of furniture can sometimes be identified.

It is a reflection of the character of English vernacular furniture in general that clock cases from the northern counties of England tend to be both more generous in their use of oak and more decorative in their treatment than those from the southern counties. It has also been noted that in northern clocks made after about 1750 the pillars at the corners of the hood (the top section of the case which contains the movement) are generally freestanding and the top of the trunk door is normally shaped in some way, whereas southern clocks tended to retain the earlier fashion for attached hood pillars and trunk doors with straight tops as late as the early nineteenth century in some instances. Other general northern features include a more widespread use of mahogany crossbanding on oak cases and (London-made clocks excepted) a greater incidence of trunk corners embellished with quarter-columns.

An eight-day longcase clock by Edward Bell of Uttoxeter, Staffordshire, c.1795. The movement of this example is fitted with a more up-to-date arched white dial. The oak case repeats many of the regional features seen on the Collier clock.

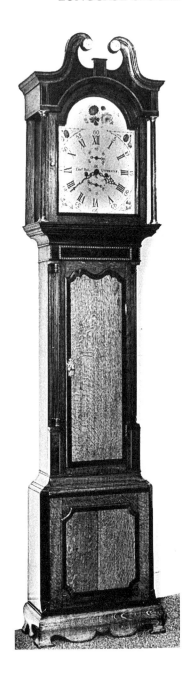

More specifically regional trends have been identified. Hood pillars having a shallow *rope-twist* decoration, for instance, are a particularly recurring feature of clocks from Cheshire and a base ornamented with imitation quoins (similar to those on buildings) is associated with late eighteenth-century clock cases from the Liverpool area. Similarly, provincial clocks having circular, as opposed to the more usual square or arched, dials tend to be found more frequently in south Yorkshire and the north Midlands than in other regions. A wavy edge to the dial aperture in the hood door is typical of clocks from the West Country.

From the early 1770s onwards the engraved brass dial was gradually superseded by japanned iron dials having a cream-white ground. These *white dials* were supplied to clockmakers by wholesale factories (centred mainly in Birmingham) and in the early nineteenth century the movements themselves were also increasingly being mass-produced by large manufacturers. After the middle of the nineteenth century the English clock industry rapidly declined in the face of competition from Germany and the United States and it was the cheap imports from these countries that were to be found in nearly every home during the late Victorian period.

An oak joined bedstead said to have been made for the grammar school at Thame, Oxfordshire, when it opened in 1570 and associated with John Hampden, the seventeenth-century statesman, who was educated there. Wheels are mounted on the feet, allowing the bedstead to be rolled sideways.

BEDROOM FURNITURE

The early courtly convention of regarding bedchambers as formal rooms suitable for receiving guests was sometimes echoed in more humble households and much expense was lavished on the hangings and covers of the bedstead. In middle-class homes of the seventeenth century the bedstead itself might be of the tester type. This had a wooden ceiling, or *tester*, which met the top of the high headboard at the back and was supported by a pair of turned posts at the foot. The main frame was strung with rope webbing to support the bedding, normally a woven mattress, a *bed* stuffed with flock or feathers, and sheets, blankets and quilt. The head of the bed would be well provided with bolsters and pillows as it was customary at this time to sleep almost in a sitting position. The *half-headed* bedstead, with a lower headboard and no tester, represented a less expensive form of bed and the simplest bedsteads were little more than boarded boxes or raised platforms. It was common for servants or children to sleep in the same room as their master or parents and they were often accommodated on a *truckle* or *trundle* bed, a low bedstead equipped with wheels which was normally stored under the main bedstead when not in use and rolled out at night. The very poor simply slept on straw pallets on the floor or on no special bedding at all.

In single-storey dwellings or those in which the upper floor was customarily given over to storage, a ground-floor bedroom was provided or the family slept in the communal kitchen/living-room. In the north of England, where such sleeping arrangements were common, privacy (and warmth) at night was often effected by building the bed behind a partition or into a recess and enclosing it behind hinged or sliding doors, normally ventilated in some way. Various methods of concealing beds were popular by the early nineteenth century and, in his *Encyclopaedia* of 1833, J. C. Loudon mentions folding 'sofa beds' and 'press bedsteads'. The latter could be compacted into what looked like a cupboard or a chest of drawers by day. Loudon noted that they were 'very common in kitchens, and, sometimes, in parlours where there is a deficiency of bed-rooms' but he had reservations: 'they are objectionable, as harbouring vermin, and being apt soon to get out of order when in daily use.' The four-poster *tent bed*, in which the posts are linked at the top by an open framework supporting a cloth canopy and curtains, was a standard form at this time but, as the nineteenth century progressed, the wooden bedstead was gradually superseded by iron and brass

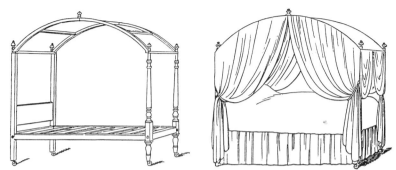

A tent bed illustrated in J. C. Loudon's 'Encyclopaedia of Cottage, Farm and Villa Architecture and Furniture' of 1833.

An oak cradle, first half of the eighteenth century.

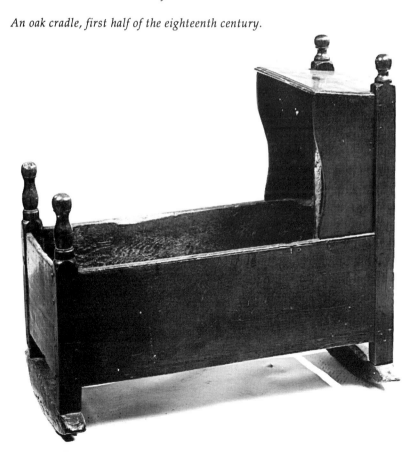

varieties. Metal bedsteads were generally cheaper than wooden types and were widely regarded as more hygienic.

The advantages of a cradle which could be rocked in order to pacify the occupant were recognised at an early date and two methods of rocking were employed from at least the fifteenth century. Either the cradle itself was fitted with curved wooden battens under the base or it was suspended on a separate stand. The body of the cradle was generally deep since it had to allow for the several layers of bedding normally used for infants in earlier times. Often, a thick underlay of loose rushes or rush matting, changed daily as it became damp, was incorporated. The baby, heavily covered by blankets and a coverlet, lay near the top of the cradle and a hooded structure was usually provided to protect its head from draughts. While most *surviving* cradles of the eighteenth century or before tend to be of superior joined construction, it seems likely that the large majority of cradles throughout the ages were boarded or of basketwork.

The luxury of a separate, purpose-built bathroom was virtually unknown in ordinary homes before the twentieth century and both toilet and washing facilities were commonly provided in the bedroom. Supplementing the garden privies, chamber pots were frequently kept in the bedroom for night-time use and could be concealed in various types of furniture. *Close* (enclosed) *stools* and *commode chairs* were often adaptations of conventional forms following the styles of the period. The seat rails were made deeper to hide the pot and the seat itself was either hinged or removable to allow access. Alternatively, the pot might be kept in a simple *pot cupboard* or *night cupboard* standing next to the bed. Jugs and basins for washing were simply kept on a convenient side table, perhaps a dressing table of the lowboy type discussed earlier, or stored on one of the stands, *washstands*, specifically designed for that purpose from the mid eighteenth century onwards. Washstand tops are occasionally pierced to hold the basin and nineteenth-century examples are normally fitted with a *splash-board*, a wooden screen around three sides of the top surface, to protect the adjacent wall from splashes. If no rails were provided on the washstand itself, towels were hung on a nearby *towel stand* or *towel horse* (often called a *towel rail* although, strictly, the rails are only the horizontal members, not the entire object). The bath was a portable metal tub kept hanging on a wall and, when required, set up in the kitchen or a bedroom, where it was laboriously filled with water by hand.

Left: An elm commode chair, probably from East Anglia, late eighteenth or early nineteenth century. The wide rails conceal a chamber pot mounted beneath the removable rush seat.
Right: A pine washstand, mid nineteenth century. The screen around the top protected the wall from splashes and the jug was kept on the shelf when not in use. This washstand comes from Lincolnshire and the late use of pegs to secure the mortise-and-tenon joints is typical of examples from this region.

Some confusion appears to have arisen from a modern misunderstanding of the old word 'press', used to describe the large cupboards in which clothes or other items were kept before the twentieth century. Too often the term is reserved exclusively for those cupboards having shelves fitted internally, since 'press' is inextricably linked in the modern mind with the idea of keeping the clothes pressed flat, but the word 'press' was, in the not too distant past, simply a synonym for 'cupboard' — any cupboard, whether fitted with shelves or not — and, in this context, had no connection with its alternative meaning, that of exerting pressure. Eighteenth-century clothes cupboards often had the base fitted with drawers and the upper part either given over entirely to hanging space, with hooks fixed around the top, or filled with shelves or sliding trays; both types were known as a 'press'. It was not until the revised use of the word 'wardrobe' (previously denoting a room rather than a piece of furniture) at the end of the eighteenth century that a distinction began to be made between different kinds of clothes presses. Some authors, including Sheraton, used 'wardrobe' to describe only those presses primarily devoted to hanging clothes; others, including Hepplewhite, applied the term to those having shelves or trays.

An oak clothes press from the Lancashire/Cheshire region, 1760-1810. This large example is over 7 feet (2.1 metres) high and would have been used in a more affluent household. The configuration of the base is similar to that of many dressers from the same region.

Large presses with shelves were not invariably regarded in the past as bedroom furniture. They were often used to store the household linen, such pieces assuming the name *linen press* during the nineteenth century, and were occasionally sited on a landing or downstairs. The Victorian wardrobe was typically a combination of hanging space — with a pull-out frame fitted with hooks at the top — on one side and a series of sliding trays on the other. The base of both sections might be filled with one or two drawers (normally intended for hats or bonnets) or a lidded compartment. It was not until the twentieth century that it became standard practice to omit hooks and, instead, to fit the top of the hanging space with a horizontal rail on which to suspend coat-hangers.

KITCHEN ARTICLES

The kitchen of the poorest type of English house was the main, and sometimes the only, downstairs room before the higher expectations for living standards that arrived with the twentieth century. In such simple homes a separate parlour was regarded as a rare luxury and the kitchen generally had to fulfil both functions; it was both the working room in which meals were cooked and eaten and the communal living-room in which family life was centred and where friends could be entertained. Pieces of furniture suitable to either kitchen or parlour were therefore typically juxtaposed in the same room and the finest family treasure — say, a mahogany longcase clock — might stand beside a crude pine bench. The lowliest room of the house, normally termed the back kitchen or wash-house, occupied a secondary downstairs chamber, sometimes in a lean-to or extension, and was given over to laundering and to preparing and storing foodstuffs and fuel. A stone or pottery sink would be found here and, if not collected from a well, water was provided during the nineteenth century by a pump or a tap connected to a mains supply. Clothes were washed in a large metal vessel, or *copper*, which was sometimes built into one corner of the room, or in a washing trough, a large wooden box having inclined sides, which normally stood on a bench or table.

A variety of specialised wooden objects were devised for the tasks of everyday life and the storage of household necessities. When not stored in the drawers of a kitchen table or dresser, cutlery was kept in standing trays, partitioned to separate knives and forks and normally provided with a carrying handle, or in trays and boxes designed to hang on a wall. Cutlery boxes were generally either made with inclined sides and a sloping lid or provided with straight sides and a front which slid upwards in grooves. The latter (but not, despite a modern belief, the former) could also be used for storing candles and were often hung near the foot of the staircase, with one or two candlesticks nearby, for convenience at bedtime. Such boxes occasionally have a small compartment at one end, in which to keep the tinder, flint and steel.

Both the fragile nature and the superior status of spoons suggested a different method of storage and they were frequently displayed hanging vertically in two or three rows on a small wall rack, each spoon being allocated an individual slot in horizontal battens. Other types of rack include those having slotted uprights designed to hold horizontally the

An oak cutlery box found
in Nottinghamshire, first
half of the nineteenth
century. This example
bears an inlaid motif of
knife and fork.

A pine plate rack, late
nineteenth or early
twentieth century.

An elm dough bin from northern England, eighteenth century. The interior of the dovetailed box is partitioned.

various spits and other iron cooking implements used on open fires. These were normally mounted above the fireplace. Racks intended for drying and storing plates and dishes were also hung on the wall or rested on a convenient surface. These were made as wooden cages, with rows of vertical spindles to keep the plates separate. Salt was an abundant commodity in most parts of England and was generally kept in a fairly large, lidded box, either wall-hanging or standing, which was sometimes partitioned so as to divide coarse and fine varieties. The design occasionally incorporates a small drawer in which to keep the spoon or to store spices. Such boxes were naturally located near the kitchen fireplace, both for convenience and for the necessity of preventing the contents from absorbing moisture.

Making bread at home was common before the twentieth century, particularly in more remote areas lacking the services of a local baker, and the task was typically performed in the back kitchen. A number of wooden hutches or *arks* intended for storing foodstuffs such as meal or

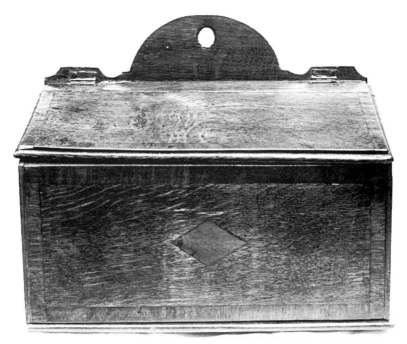

Oak hanging box probably for storing salt, first half of the nineteenth century.

flour survive from the sixteenth and seventeenth centuries but most extant examples of this age are likely to have originated in larger farmhouses or more affluent homes. These receptacles are of an archaic chest-like form and tend to have removable canted lids which can be inverted and used as a trough in which to knead dough. Later dough bins, or *kneading troughs*, are typically simple boxes, having inclined sides, which are supported on four legs tied by stretchers and provided with a flat lid. Those of the nineteenth century were clearly described by Loudon in 1833: 'The cover, which, when on the trough, serves as a table or ironing-board, either lifts off, or, being hinged, is placed so as when opened it may lean against a wall ... Frequently a division is made in the centre of the trough, so that the dry flour can be kept in one compartment, and the dough made in the other.'

FURTHER READING

There are relatively few books devoted exclusively to the history of English vernacular furniture. The following selection includes not only books on the subject as a whole and those dealing with specific aspects (such as chairs or longcase clocks) but also one or two of the more important general furniture books and works which, while devoted primarily to other topics, contain relevant material. Studies of foreign (for example Welsh, Irish and North American) vernacular furniture are recognised as highly significant since they relate to the English tradition. Especially important, though too numerous to list here, are articles in various periodicals and the publications of the Furniture History Society (founded in 1964) and the Regional Furniture Society (founded in 1986).

Ayres, James. *The Shell Book of the Home in Britain*. Faber & Faber, 1981.

Bly, John. *Discovering English Furniture*. Shire, 1976, reprinted 1993.

Chinnery, Victor. *Oak Furniture. The British Tradition*. Antique Collectors' Club, Woodbridge, 1979.

Cotton, Bernard D. *The English Regional Chair*. Antique Collectors' Club, Woodbridge, 1990.

Crispin, Thomas. *The English Windsor Chair*. Alan Sutton, Stroud, 1992.

Filbee, Marjorie. *Dictionary of Country Furniture*. The Connoisseur, 1977.

Gilbert, Christopher. *English Vernacular Furniture 1750-1900*. Yale University Press, 1991.

Goodman, W. L. *The History of Woodworking Tools*. G. Bell & Sons, 1964.

Hayden, Arthur. *Chats on Cottage and Farmhouse Furniture*. Benn, 1950 (first edition 1912).

Jekyll, Gertrude, and Jones, Sydney R. *Old English Household Life*. Batsford, 1945 (first edition 1925).

Kirk, John T. *American Furniture and the British Tradition to 1830*. Alfred A. Knopf, New York, 1982.

Knell, David. *English Country Furniture*. Barrie & Jenkins, 1992.

Loomes, Brian. *Grandfather Clocks and their Cases*. David & Charles, Newton Abbot, 1985.

Loughnan, Nicholas. *Irish Country Furniture*. Eason & Son, Dublin, 1984.

Macquoid, Percy. *A History of English Furniture*. Studio Editions, 1991 (first edition 1904-8).

Macquoid, Percy, and Edwards, Ralph. *The Dictionary of English Furniture*. Antique Collectors' Club, Woodbridge, 1986 (first edition 1924-7).

Pain, Howard. *The Heritage of Upper Canadian Furniture.* Van Nostrand Reinhold, Toronto, 1978.

Pinto, Edward H. *Treen and Other Wooden Bygones.* G. Bell & Sons, 1969.

Roe, F. Gordon. *English Cottage Furniture.* Phoenix, 1949.

Roe, F. Gordon. *Windsor Chairs.* Phoenix, 1953.

Sparkes, Ivan. *The English Country Chair.* Spurbooks, 1973.

Sparkes, Ivan. *The Windsor Chair.* Spurbooks, 1975.

Sparkes, Ivan. *English Windsor Chairs.* Shire, 1981, reprinted 1989.

Toller, Jane. *Country Furniture.* David & Charles, Newton Abbot, 1973.

Twiston-Davies, L., and Lloyd-Johnes, H. J. *Welsh Furniture.* University of Wales Press, 1950.

Places to Visit

Examples of vernacular furniture are included in the collections of the following museums and houses open to the public. Intending visitors are advised to telephone before making a special journey to ensure that relevant items are on display and to ascertain the times of opening.

Serious enthusiasts might consider joining the Regional Furniture Society (Membership Secretary, Trouthouse, Warrens Cross, Lechlade, Gloucestershire GL7 3DR).

AVON
American Museum in Britain, Claverton Manor, Bath BA2 7BD. Telephone: 0225 460503. American furniture.

BEDFORDSHIRE
Elstow Moot Hall, Elstow, Bedford. Telephone: 0234 228330.

BERKSHIRE
Museum of English Rural Life, The University, Whiteknights, Reading RG6 2AG. Telephone: 0734 318660.

BUCKINGHAMSHIRE
Chiltern Open Air Museum, Newland Park, Gorelands Lane, Chalfont St Giles HP8 4AD. Telephone: 0494 871117.
Wycombe Local History and Chair Museum, Castle Hill House, Priory Avenue, High Wycombe. Telephone: 0494 421895

CHESHIRE
Quarry Bank Mill, Styal SK9 4LA. Telephone: 0625 527468.

CUMBRIA
Museum of Lakeland Life and Industry, Abbot Hall, Kendal LA9 5AL. Telephone: 0539 722464.
Townend, Troutbeck, Windermere LA23 1LB. Telephone: 05394 32628. National Trust.

DERBYSHIRE
Haddon Hall, Bakewell DE4 1LA. Telephone: 0629 812855.

DEVON
Elizabethan House, 32 New Street, Plymouth PL1 2NA. Telephone: 0752 668000 extension 4380.
St Anne's Chapel and Old Grammar School Museum, St Peter's Churchyard, Barnstaple. Telephone: 0271 78709 or 46747.

DORSET
Dorset County Museum, High West Street, Dorchester DT1 1XA. Telephone: 0305 262735.
Priest's House Museum, 23-27 High Street, Wimborne Minster BH21 1HR. Telephone: 0202 882533.

DURHAM
Beamish: The North of England Open Air Museum, Beamish DH9 0RG. Telephone: 0207 231811.
The Bowes Museum, Barnard Castle DL12 8NP. Telephone: 0833 690606.

EAST SUSSEX
Anne of Cleves House Museum, 52 Southover High Street, Lewes BN7 1JA. Telephone: 0273 474610.
Michelham Priory, Upper Dicker, Hailsham BN27 3QS. Telephone: 0323 844224.

ESSEX
Southchurch Hall, Southchurch Hall Close, Southend-on-Sea. Telephone: 0702 467671.

GLOUCESTERSHIRE
Gloucester Folk Museum, 99-103 Westgate Street, Gloucester GL1 2PG. Telephone: 0452 526467.

GREATER LONDON
Geffrye Museum, Kingsland Road, Shoreditch, London E2 8EA. Telephone: 071-739 9893.
Museum of London, London Wall, London EC2Y 5HN. Telephone: 071-600 3699.
Victoria and Albert Museum, Cromwell Road, South Kensington, London SW7 2RL. Telephone: 071-938 8500.

GREATER MANCHESTER
Hall i'th' Wood Museum, Green Way, off Crompton Way, Bolton BL1 8UA. Telephone: 0204 301159.
Ordsall Hall Museum, Taylorson Street, Salford M5 3EX. Telephone: 061-872 0251.
Wythenshawe Hall, Wythenshawe Park, Northenden, Manchester M23 0AB. Telephone: 061-236 5244.

HAMPSHIRE
Breamore House, Breamore, Fordingbridge SP6 2DF. Telephone: 0725 22468.
Portsmouth City Museum, Museum Road, Old Portsmouth PO1 2LJ. Telephone: 0705 827261 or 296906.

HEREFORD AND WORCESTER
The Old House, High Town, Hereford. Telephone: 0432 268121 extension 225.

HUMBERSIDE
Hornsea Museum, Burns Farm, 11 Newbegin, Hornsea HU18 1AB. Telephone: 0964 533443.
Wilberforce House and Georgian Houses, High Street, Hull. Telephone: 0482 593902.

LANCASHIRE
Astley Hall Museum and Art Gallery, Astley Park, Chorley PR7 1NP. Telephone: 0257 262166.
Cottage Museum, 15 Castle Hill, Lancaster. Telephone: 0524 64637.
Towneley Hall Art Gallery and Museums, Burnley BB11 3RQ. Telephone: 0282 24213.

LINCOLNSHIRE
Boston Guildhall Museum, South Street, Boston PE21 6HT. Telephone: 0205 365954.
Gainsborough Old Hall, Parnell Street, Gainsborough, DN21 2NB. Telephone: 0427 612669.
Museum of Lincolnshire Life, The Old Barracks, Burton Road, Lincoln LN1 3LY. Telephone: 0522 528448.

MERSEYSIDE
Speke Hall, The Walk, Speke, Liverpool L24 1XD. Telephone: 051-427 7231.

NORFOLK
Elizabethan House Museum, 4 South Quay, Great Yarmouth NR30 2QH. Telephone: 0493 855746.
Museum of Lynn Life, 46 Queen Street, King's Lynn PE30 5DQ. Telephone: 0553 773450.
Norfolk Rural Life Museum, Beech House, Gressenhall, Dereham NR20 4DR. Telephone: 0362 860563.
Old Merchant's House and Row 111 Houses, South Quay, Great Yarmouth NR30 2RQ. Telephone: 0493 857900.
Strangers' Hall Museum, Charing Cross, Norwich NR2 4AL. Telephone: 0603 667229.

NORTH YORKSHIRE
Ryedale Folk Museum, Hutton-le-Hole YO6 6UA. Telephone: 07515 367.
York Castle Museum, Tower Street, York YO1 1RY. Telephone: 0904 653611.

SHROPSHIRE
Ironbridge Gorge Museum, Ironbridge, Telford TF8 7AW. Telephone: 0952 433522.

STAFFORDSHIRE
Ford Green Hall, Ford Green Road, Smallthorne, Stoke-on-Trent ST6 1NG. Telephone: 0782 534771.

SUFFOLK
Christchurch Mansion, Christchurch Park, Ipswich IP1 3QH. Telephone: 0473 213761 or 253246.
Museum of East Anglian Life, Stowmarket IP14 1DL. Telephone 0449 612229.

TYNE AND WEAR
Washington Old Hall, Washington. Telephone: 091-416 6879. National Trust.

WARWICKSHIRE
Shakespeare Birthplace Trust, The Shakespeare Centre, Henley Street, Stratford-upon-Avon CV37 6QW. Telephone: 0789 204016. The trust administers these properties in and around Stratford-upon-Avon: Shakespeare's Birthplace, Henley Street; Anne Hathaway's Cottage, Shottery; New Place and Nash' s House, Chapel Street; Hall's Croft, Old Town; Mary Arden's House and Shakespeare Countryside Museum, Wilmcote; Harvard House, High Street.

WEST MIDLANDS
Aston Hall, Trinity Road, Aston, Birmingham. Telephone: 021-327 0062.
Black Country Museum, Tipton Road, Dudley DY1 4SQ. Telephone: 021-557 9643.

WEST SUSSEX
The Priest House, West Hoathly, East Grinstead RH19 4PP. Telephone: 0342 810479.
St Mary's House, Bramber, Steyning. Telephone: 0903 816205.

WEST YORKSHIRE
Bolling Hall, Bowling Hall Road, Bradford BD4 7LP. Telephone: 0274 723057.
Calderdale Industrial Museum, The Piece Hall, Halifax HX1 1RE. Telephone: 0422 358087.
Heptonstall Museum, Old Grammar School, Churchyard Bottom, Heptonstall, Hebden Bridge. Telephone: 0422 843738. School furniture.
Oakwell Hall, Nutter Lane, Birstall, Batley WF17 9LG. Telephone: 0924 474926.
Shibden Hall and Folk Museum of West Yorkshire, Shibden Hall, Listers Road, Halifax HX3 6XG. Telephone: 0422 352246.
Temple Newsam House, Leeds LS15 0AE. Telephone: 0532 641358 or 647321.

INDEX

Page numbers in italic refer to illustrations